Yu-Gi-Oh!

TRADING CARD GAME

Card Catalog

Prima's Official Strategy Guide

Prima Games
A Division of Random House, Inc.

3000 Lava Ridge Court
Roseville, CA 95661
(800) 733-3000
www.primagames.com

Project Editor: Teli Hernandez

© 1996 KAZUKI TAKAHASHI.
Konami is a registered trademark of KONAMI CORPORATION.
© 2003 KONAMI & Konami Computer Entertainment Japan.

All products and characters mentioned in this book are trademarks of their respective companies.

Please be advised that the ESRB rating icons, "EC", "K-A", "E", "T", "M", "AO" and "RP" are copyrighted works and certification marks owned by the Interactive Digital Software Association and may only be used with their permission and authority. Under no circumstances may the rating icons be self applied or used in connection with any product that has not been rated by the ESRB. For information regarding whether a product that has no been rated by the ESRB, please call the ESRB at 1-800-771-3772 or visit www.esrb.org. For information regarding licensing issues, please call IDSA at (212)223-8936. Please note that ESRB ratings only apply to the content of the game itself and does NOT apply to the content of this book.

Important:
Prima Games has made every effort to determine that the information contained in this book is accurate. However, the publisher makes no warranty, either expressed or implied, as to the accuracy, effectiveness, or completeness of the material in this book; nor does the publisher assume liability for damages, either incidental or consequential, that may result from using the information in this book. The publisher cannot provide information regarding game play, hints and strategies, or problems with hardware or software. Questions should be directed to the support numbers provided by the game and device manufacturers in their documentation. Some game tricks require precise timing and may require repeated attempts before the desired result is achieved.

ISBN: 0-7615-3942-5
Library of Congress Catalog Card Number: 2002103848
Printed in the United States of America

03 04 05 06 GG 10 9 8 7 6 5 4 3 2 1

Contents

Official Rules

This is an introduction to the Official Rules for the *Yu-Gi-Oh! TRADING CARD GAME*. For complete rules, see the Official Rulebook included with all Starter Decks.

Preparing Your Deck

Your Starter Deck contains all the cards you'll need to challenge an opponent to a Duel. In the following list you'll find basic rules for preparing your Deck.

- The Deck used for Dueling should contain a minimum of 40 cards. Aside from this minimum limit, your Deck can contain as many cards as you'd like.
- In addition to your Dueling Deck, you can also have 15 additional cards in a separate pile, known as the Side Deck. The Side Deck allows you to modify your Deck to better suit your strategy during a Match.

Between Duels, you can exchange any card from your Side Deck with any card in your Deck—as long as you end up with the same number of cards that your Deck began the Match with.

The Side Deck you create must contain exactly 15 cards at the beginning of a Match. In other words, if you don't have enough cards to create a 15-card Side Deck, you cannot use one at all.

In any Match, the Deck and Side Deck combined cannot contain more than three copies of the same card. Also, be aware of Forbidden and Limited Cards.

Preparing to Fight

You need the following items to start:
- Deck of *Yu-Gi-Oh! TCG* cards (made up of at least 40 cards)
- Game Mat

Game Mat

While battling, lay cards that you play and throw away onto the Game Mat.

Gameplay

In accordance with the Official Rules, a Duel is conducted in the following manner:

- Before you start a Duel, greet your opponent with a friendly handshake.
- Both players shuffle their respective Decks and hand them to their opponent to shuffle (this is called Cutting the Deck). The Decks are then returned to their owners and placed face-down in their respective Deck Zones on the Game Mat.
- When using Fusion Monster Cards, place the cards face-down on the Fusion Deck Zone of the Game Mat. A Fusion Deck is a card or a group of cards consisting only of Fusion Monsters formed by fusing two or more Monsters during a Duel.
- Show your opponent that your Side Deck contains exactly 15 cards (the cards may be counted face-down). When your Side Deck cards are exchanged with those in your Deck, count the cards in your Side Deck again to verify that the Deck still contains the same number of cards.

- For the first Duel in a Match, decide who starts first with a coin toss. Whoever wins the coin toss, can decide to go first or second. For subsequent Duels in the Match, the loser of the previous Duel decides who starts first. If the previous Duel ended in a tie, re-toss a coin to determine who starts first in the next Duel.
- Finally, each player draws five cards from the top of their respective Decks. Once both players have five cards in their hand, the Duel begins.

Manners in Dueling

Remember the following codes of conduct when facing an opponent:
- Always declare each move in a loud, clear voice before you execute any play.
- Your opponent is entitled to know the content of your Graveyard and the number of cards in your hand. If asked, you are obliged to answer truthfully.
- Never touch an opponent's cards without asking permission.

Objective of the Game

Follow these Official Rules when waging battle:
- The objective of the *Yu-Gi-Oh! TCG* is to win a Match against your opponent.
- A single Match consists of three Duels. Each card battle against an opponent in which a win, loss, or draw is determined is referred to as a Duel.
- The first person to win two Duels or has one win and two draws in a Match wins that Match.
- A Match with Duels that result in one win, one loss, and one draw or three draws is a draw Match, and no one wins or loses.

Winning a Duel

The outcome of a Duel is decided according to the following Official Rules:
- Each player begins a Duel with 8,000 Life Points.
- Life Points decrease as a result of damage calculation after battle. You win a Duel if you reduce your opponent's Life Points to zero. If your opponent reduces your Life Points to zero, YOU lose!
- If you and your opponent both reach zero Life Points at the same time, the Duel is declared a draw.
- If either player's Deck runs out of cards during a Duel, the first player unable to draw a card is declared the loser. Bearing this in mind, a good Duelist should make every card count.
- If at any time during the Duel you hold the following cards in your hand, you instantly win the Duel:
    "Right Leg of the Forbidden One"
    "Left Leg of the Forbidden One"
    "Right Arm of the Forbidden One"
    "Left Arm of the Forbidden One"
    "Exodia the Forbidden One"

Phases of Gameplay

Draw Phase
Draw one card from the top of your Deck on your turn.

Standby Phase
If there are any cards in play on the Field that specifically state that certain actions must be taken during this phase, these must be dealt with prior to entering the Main Phase. Refer to the cards for specific details regarding the actions to be taken. If there are no such cards in play, proceed to Main Phase 1.

Main Phase 1
During this phase, you may: (1) Normal Summon or Set one Monster Card, (2) activate and/or Set Spell Cards, and (3) Set Trap Cards. Keep in mind that you may not exceed the five-card limit for the Monster Card Zone or the Spell & Trap Card Zone.

During this phase, you may also change the Attack or Defense Position of cards placed on the Field during a previous turn. The postion of each card can be changed only once in a single turn, during either Main Phase 1 or 2. However, remember that once a Monster attacks, it cannot be changed to Defense Position in the same turn.

IMPORTANT! You CANNOT change the Battle Position (Attack to Defense Position or vice-vesa) of a Monster Card during the same turn in which it has been Summoned or Set.

At the end of the Main Phase 1, you can choose to enter the Battle Phase or proceed to the End Phase (the starting player cannot conduct a Battle Phase in their first turn).

Battle Phase
The Battle Phase consists of the following four steps:

Start Step: Declare that you are entering the Battle Phase. You and your opponent may both play Quick-Play Spell and/or Trap Cards.

Battle Step: Select and announce one Monster to attack with, and declare one of your opponent's Monsters your target (the Monster you wish to attack). You and your opponent may both play Quick-Play Spell and/or Trap Cards.

Damage Step: Calculate the damage points of the designated Monsters. If a Monster has a Flip Effect, apply it immediately after damage calculation. However, a Flip Effect does not affect Monsters that have already been destroyed as a result of damage calculation.

End Step: Resolve all battles by repeating the Battle and Damage Steps as many times as necessary, then declare an end to your Battle Phase. You and your opponent may both play Quick-Play Spell and/or Trap Cards.

Determining Damage

When the Opponent's Monster is in Attack Position
When the Monster you attack is also in the Attack Position, determine the damage by comparing the ATK of the two Monsters.

If the ATK of your attacking Monster are greater than the ATK of your opponent's Monster, your opponent's Monster is destroyed. Subtract the value of the ATK of your opponent's Monster from the ATK of your Monster. Deduct the result from your opponent's Life Points.

If the ATK of your Monster are the same as your opponent's Monster, the battle is a draw, and both Monsters are destroyed. Neither player receives damage, resulting in no change in Life Points.

If the ATK of your Monster are less than the ATK of your opponent's Monster, your Monster is destroyed. Subtract the value of the ATK of your Monster from the ATK of your opponent's Monster. Deduct the result from your Life Points.

When the Opponent's Monster Is in Defense Position
When the Monster you attack is in the Defense Position, determine the damage by comparing the ATK of your Monster with the DEF of the Monster you are attacking.

If the ATK of your attacking Monster are greater than the DEF of your opponent's Monster, destroy your opponent's Monster. Neither player receives damage, resulting in no change in Life Points.

If the ATK of your Monster are the same as the DEF of your opponent's Monster, neither Monster is destroyed. Neither player receives damage, resulting in no change in Life Points.

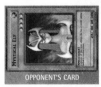

If the ATK of your Monster are less than the DEF of your opponent's Monster, neither Monster is destroyed. Subtract the value of the ATK of your Monster from the DEF of your opponent's Monster. Deduct the result from your Life Points.

When the Opponent Has No Monsters on the Field

If no enemy Monster Cards exist on the Field, your opponent receives Direct Damage. Deduct the attacking Monster's ATK from your opponent's Life Points.

Main Phase 2

When the Battle Phase is over, the turn proceeds to Main Phase 2. As in Main Phase 1, you may Set or play Monster, Spell, and/or Trap Cards. Remember that you are allowed to change the Attack or Defense Position of each Monster or perform a Normal Summon only ONCE PER TURN. Remember that if a Monster attacks in the Battle Phase, it may not be changed to Defense Position in the same turn. Also keep in mind that you may not exceed the five-card limit for the Monster Card Zone or the Spell & Trap Card Zone.

End Phase

Announce the end of your turn. If your hand contains more than six cards, discard to the Graveyard until only six cards remain in your hand. The opposing player then begins his/her turn with the Draw Phase.

Concluding a Duel

Continue the steps from the Draw Phase to the End Phase until a winner is decided. This happens when one player's points reach zero, can no longer draw a card from his Deck when required to draw, or holds all five Exodia cards in his hand, and the Duel comes to an end.

Game Cards

Three main card types are used in *Yu-Gi-Oh! TCG:* Monster Cards, Spell Cards, and Trap Cards. Additionally, each type of card is divided into further sub-categories. For now, just read the card descriptions. After familiarizing yourself with the "Phases of Gameplay" section, you will understand the special role of each of the cards.

Monster Cards

A Monster Card is the basic card used to attack your opponent. Monster Cards are categorized by Type and Attribute. There are 20 different Types and six different Atttributes. Type and Attribute affect each Monster's ability to attack and defend.

The overall strength of a Monster is indicated by its Level (the number of stars at the upper right of the Monster Card). Also note that the italicized text in the card description box is descriptive text only, and has NO effect on gameplay.

MONSTER NAME
ATTRIBUTE
LEVEL
TYPE
CARD DESCRIPTION
ATK (Attack Points)
DEF (Defense Points)

Other than Normal Monster Cards, there are also Fusion Monster Cards, Ritual Monster Cards, Effect Monster Cards, and Monster Tokens. Please refer to the Official Rulebook for more details.

Spell Cards

There are several types of Spell cards. Spell Cards can only be activated or Set during Main Phases. The only exception to the rule are Quick-Play Spell Cards.

Spell Cards types are indentified by card icons. Spell Cards are color-coded GREEN.

There are Normal Spell Cards, Continuous Spell Cards, Equip Spell Cards, Field Spell Cards, Quick-Play Spell Cards, and Ritual Spell Cards. Please refer to the Official Rulebook for more details.

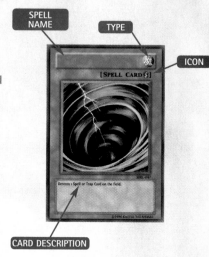

SPELL NAME
TYPE
ICON
CARD DESCRIPTION

Trap Cards

You can Set these cards on the Field and activate them at any time after the start of the next turn providing the requirements for activating the Trap Card have been met. Trap Card types are identified by card icons. Trap Cards are color-coded PURPLE.

There are Normal Trap Cards, Counter Trap Cards, and Continuous Trap Cards. Please refer to the Official Rulebook for more details.

TRAP NAME
TYPE
ICON
CARD DESCRIPTION

Starter Deck Yugi

SDY-001 Mystical Elf

Card Type: Normal Monster
Monster Type: Spellcaster
Attribute: Light
Level: 4
ATK: 800
DEF: 2000
Rarity: Common

Rely on "Mystical Elf" for defense. However, since she has low ATK, she's easy prey for "Fissure...."

SDY-002 Feral Imp

Card Type: Normal Monster
Monster Type: Fiend
Attribute: Dark
Level: 4
ATK: 1300
DEF: 1400
Rarity: Common

This small Fiend's entire body is colored green. Its love of practical jokes makes it troublesome to deal with.

SDY-003 Winged Dragon, Guardian of the Fortress #1

Card Type: Normal Monster
Monster Type: Dragon
Attribute: Wind
Level: 4
ATK: 1400
DEF: 1200
Rarity: Common

Mountain battles are this Dragon's specialty. It frustrates enemies with sneak attacks!

SDY-004 Summoned Skull

Card Type: Normal Monster
Monster Type: Fiend
Attribute: Dark
Level: 6
ATK: 2500
DEF: 1200
Rarity: Common

Though "Summoned Skull" is a high-level Fiend, it's easy to Summon and extremely useful.

SDY-005 Beaver Warrior

Card Type: Normal Monster
Monster Type: Beast-Warrior
Attribute: Earth
Level: 4
ATK: 1200
DEF: 1500
Rarity: Common

"Beaver Warrior" is one of Yugi's favorite Beast-Warriors. Set this Monster first in Defense Position, then switch it to Attack Position when you see an opening!

SDY-006 Dark Magician

Card Type: Normal Monster
Monster Type: Spellcaster
Attribute: Dark
Level: 7
ATK: 2500
DEF: 2100
Rarity: Ultra Rare

A high-ranking magician of the Spellcaster-Type, the "Dark Magician" is very dangerous unless you destroy him as soon as your opponent places him on the Field.

SDY-007 Gaia The Fierce Knight

Card Type: Normal Monster
Monster Type: Warrior
Attribute: Earth
Level: 7
ATK: 2300
DEF: 2100
Rarity: Common

Yugi uses this top-class Warrior. Don't fail to include this card in a Warrior-Type Deck!

SDY-008 Curse of Dragon

Card Type: Normal Monster
Monster Type: Dragon
Attribute: Dark
Level: 5
ATK: 2000
DEF: 1500
Rarity: Common

This cursed Dragon chars everything with its breath of flame. Instead of Setting it in Defense Position, attack!

SDY-009 Celtic Guardian

Card Type:
Normal Monster

Monster Type:
Warrior

Attribute:
Earth

Level: **4**

ATK: **1400**

DEF: **1200**

Rarity:
Common

With high ATK, "Celtic Guardian" is an elite Warrior. He slices his enemies with his skilled techniques!

SDY-010 Mammoth Graveyard

Card Type:
Normal Monster

Monster Type:
Dinosaur

Attribute:
Earth

Level: **3**

ATK: **1200**

DEF: **800**

Rarity:
Common

Even Yugi uses this Dinosaur-Type Card. It has balanced ATK!

SDY-011 Great White

Card Type:
Normal Monster

Monster Type:
Fish

Attribute:
Water

Level: **4**

ATK: **1600**

DEF: **800**

Rarity:
Common

The main Monster of Fish-Type Monsters, its high ATK rivals "Rogue Doll's!"

SDY-012 Silver Fang

Card Type:
Normal Monster

Monster Type:
Beast

Attribute:
Earth

Level: **3**

ATK: **1200**

DEF: **800**

Rarity:
Common

Yugi often uses this feral wolf in Duels. Power it up and defeat your opponent!

SDY-013 Giant Soldier of Stone

Card Type:
Normal Monster

Monster Type:
Rock

Attribute:
Earth

Level: **3**

ATK: **1300**

DEF: **2000**

Rarity:
Common

This card will be the main Monster in a Rock-Type Deck. For a Level 3 Monster, the ATK and DEF are amazing!

SDY-014 Dragon Zombie

Card Type:
Normal Monster

Monster Type:
Zombie

Attribute:
Dark

Level: **3**

ATK: **1600**

DEF: **0**

Rarity:
Common

Magical powers revived this Zombie from the grave. It used to be a Dragon, but no one knows which one.

SDY-015 Doma The Angel of Silence

Card Type:
Normal Monster

Monster Type:
Fairy

Attribute:
Dark

Level: **5**

ATK: **1600**

DEF: **1400**

Rarity:
Common

A Fairy with DARK, this creature is full of mystery. You must offer one Monster as a Tribute to Summon this Monster.

SDY-016 Ansatsu

Card Type:
Normal Monster

Monster Type:
Warrior

Attribute:
Earth

Level: **5**

ATK: **1700**

DEF: **1200**

Rarity:
Common

When powered up by "Invigoration," this high-level Warrior can even defeat the "Mystical Elf!"

SDY-017 Witty Phantom

Card Type:
Normal Monster

Monster Type:
Fiend

Attribute:
Dark

Level: **4**

ATK: **1400**

DEF: **1300**

Rarity:
Common

This Fiend is a hard-working nice guy and is quite popular with the ladies of the underworld.

SDY-018 Claw Reacher

Card Type: Normal Monster
Monster Type: Fiend
Attribute: Dark
Level: 3
ATK: 1000
DEF: 800
Rarity: Common

This Fiend can instantly extend its arms like a machine, but its abilities are low.

SDY-019 Mystic Clown

Card Type: Normal Monster
Monster Type: Fiend
Attribute: Dark
Level: 4
ATK: 1500
DEF: 1000
Rarity: Common

Though not as powerful as "Rogue Doll," this low-level Monster has high ATK, making it a dangerous force!

SDY-020 Sword of Dark Destruction

Card Type: Spell
Monster Type: —
Attribute: Spell
Level: —
ATK: —
DEF: —
Rarity: Common

This Equip Spell Card can be equipped on any type of Monster as long as it has DARK. You'll want this card in your Deck!

SDY-021 Book of Secret Arts

Card Type: Spell
Monster Type: —
Attribute: Spell
Level: —
ATK: —
DEF: —
Rarity: Common

Use this book on "Dark Magician" to easily destroy every Monster Card, except "Blue-Eyes White Dragon!"

SDY-022 Dark Hole

Card Type: Spell
Monster Type: —
Attribute: Spell
Level: —
ATK: —
DEF: —
Rarity: Common

"Dark Hole" is very effective when the Duel is deadlocked against an opponent who is using Monsters with high DEF!

SDY-023 Dian Keto the Cure Master

Card Type: Spell
Monster Type: —
Attribute: Spell
Level: —
ATK: —
DEF: —
Rarity: Common

This motherly goddess will refill 1000 Life Points. If you have three of this card in your Deck, you can regain 3000 Life Points.

SDY-024 Ancient Elf

Card Type: Normal Monster
Monster Type: Spellcaster
Attribute: Light
Level: 4
ATK: 1450
DEF: 1200
Rarity: Common

Rumors say this elf has lived for millenniums.

SDY-025 Magical Ghost

Card Type: Normal Monster
Monster Type: Zombie
Attribute: Dark
Level: 4
ATK: 1300
DEF: 1400
Rarity: Common

A magician combined with a ghost to revive herself from the afterlife. She attacks with spells that attack her opponent's confidence.

SDY-026 Fissure

Card Type: Spell

Monster Type: —

Attribute: Spell

Level: —

ATK: —

DEF: —

Rarity: Common

This card affects face-up Monster Cards. Even the mightiest Monster Cards cannot escape this effect!

SDY-027 Trap Hole

Card Type: Trap

Monster Type: —

Attribute: Trap

Level: —

ATK: —

DEF: —

Rarity: Common

Activate "Trap Hole" when your opponent Normal Summons or Flip Summons a Monster!

SDY-028 Two-Pronged Attack

Card Type: Trap

Monster Type: —

Attribute: Trap

Level: —

ATK: —

DEF: —

Rarity: Common

"Two-Pronged Attack" is very useful when you have many Monsters on your Field. Use it as soon as your opponent Summons a powerful Monster!

SDY-029 De-Spell

Card Type: Spell

Monster Type: —

Attribute: Spell

Level: —

ATK: —

DEF: —

Rarity: Common

This Spell Card can even destroy face-down Spell Cards. If the chosen face-down card is a Trap Card, then return the Trap Card back to normal.

SDY-030 Monster Reborn

Card Type: Spell

Monster Type: —

Attribute: Spell

Level: —

ATK: —

DEF: —

Rarity: Common

If there's a Monster Card in the Graveyard, use this Spell Card to resurrect it and make it part of your team! This is an extremely important card!

SDY-031 Reinforcements

Card Type: Trap

Monster Type: —

Attribute: Trap

Level: —

ATK: —

DEF: —

Rarity: Common

Put a weak Monster in Attack Position, and use this Trap Card when your opponent attacks. It's a counterattack!

SDY-032 Change of Heart

Card Type: Spell

Monster Type: —

Attribute: Spell

Level: —

ATK: —

DEF: —

Rarity: Common

The heart is a transient thing, and this is true for Monsters' hearts as well—so much that Monsters at times forget who their masters are. The Monster you worked so hard to Summon suddenly defects to your opponent. This effect lasts only the turn "Change of Heart" is activated, so the Monster is often offered as a Tribute.

SDY-033 The Stern Mystic

Card Type: Effect Monster

Monster Type: Spellcaster

Attribute: Light

Level: 4

ATK: 1500

DEF: 1200

Rarity: Common

This card allows you to see all face-down Monster, Spell, and Trap Cards. If you know what cards your opponent is playing, you can easily prepare countermeasures.

Card Catalog

SDY-034 Wall of Illusion

Card Type: Effect Monster
Monster Type: Fiend
Attribute: Dark
Level: 4
ATK: 1000
DEF: 1850
Rarity: Common

There are few Level 4 and below Monsters that can defeat 1850 DEF. The Monsters that can defeat "Wall of Illusion" are usually Tribute Summoned Monsters, but they will be returned to your opponent's hand if they attack "Wall of Illusion."

SDY-035 Neo the Magic Swordsman

Card Type: Normal Monster
Monster Type: Spellcaster
Attribute: Light
Level: 4
ATK: 1700
DEF: 1000
Rarity: Common

This Monster has the LIGHT, but since it is also a Spellcaster, it will be powered up by the Yami Field Spell Card.

SDY-036 Baron of the Fiend Sword

Card Type: Normal Monster
Monster Type: Fiend
Attribute: Dark
Level: 4
ATK: 1550
DEF: 800
Rarity: Common

This card will power up in the Yami Field.

SDY-037 Man-Eating Treasure Chest

Card Type: Normal Monster
Monster Type: Fiend
Attribute: Dark
Level: 4
ATK: 1600
DEF: 1000
Rarity: Common

This Monster has 1600 ATK, but it will power up even further in the Yami Field.

SDY-038 Sorcerer of the Doomed

Card Type: Normal Monster
Monster Type: Spellcaster
Attribute: Dark
Level: 4
ATK: 1450
DEF: 1200
Rarity: Common

This Spellcaster is an expert in extermination spells, but its ATK and DEF may not help save his own life.

SDY-039 Last Will

Card Type: Spell
Monster Type: —
Attribute: Spell
Level: —
ATK: —
DEF: —
Rarity: Common

Don't make the mistake of thinking this card is useless because you can only Summon Monsters 1500 ATK and below. With this card, you can Summon Effect Monster Cards that hold the key to a combo.

SDY-040 Waboku

Card Type: Trap
Monster Type: —
Attribute: Trap
Level: —
ATK: —
DEF: —
Rarity: Common

Zero battle damage means that the effects of "White Magical Hat" or "Robbin' Goblin" disappear. However, "Waboku's" effect lasts for only one turn.

SDY-041 Soul Exchange

Card Type: Spell
Monster Type: —
Attribute: Spell
Level: —
ATK: —
DEF: —
Rarity: Super Rare

You cannot attack this turn, but you will use your opponent's Monster for a Tribute Summon.

SDY-042 Card Destruction

Card Type: Spell
Monster Type: —
Attribute: Spell
Level: —
ATK: —
DEF: —
Rarity: Super Rare

This card is especially useful when you have no useful cards in your hand while your opponent has many powerful cards in his or her hand.

TRADING CARD GAME

SDY-043 Trap Master

Card Type: Effect Monster

Monster Type: Warrior

Attribute: Earth

Level: 3

ATK: 500

DEF: 1100

Rarity: Common

You can destroy your opponent's Trap Card without it activating. It may be fun to Set this Monster on your first turn. It will baffle your opponent and throw his or her game off-track.

SDY-044 Dragon Capture Jar

Card Type: Trap

Monster Type: —

Attribute: Trap

Level: —

ATK: —

DEF: —

Rarity: Common

Dragon-Types should be wary of this Trap Card. Even the "Stop Defense" Spell Card can't affect "Dragon Capture Jar!"

SDY-045 Yami

Card Type: Spell

Monster Type: —

Attribute: Spell

Level: —

ATK: —

DEF: —

Rarity: Common

Since Fairy-Type Monsters crave the light, they're weak in Yami terrain. However, this terrain strengthens Fiend- and Spellcaster-Type Monsters who thrive on magical powers!

SDY-046 Man-Eater Bug

Card Type: Effect Monster

Monster Type: Insect

Attribute: Earth

Level: 2

ATK: 450

DEF: 600

Rarity: Common

If "Man-Eater Bug" is the only Monster on the Field, its effect will destroy the "Man-Eater Bug" itself....

SDY-047 Reverse Trap

Card Type: Trap

Monster Type: —

Attribute: Trap

Level: —

ATK: —

DEF: —

Rarity: Common

This card counteracts all the Spell Cards and the like that are powering up Monsters. This is a scary Trap Card!

SDY-048 Remove Trap

Card Type: Spell

Monster Type: —

Attribute: Spell

Level: —

ATK: —

DEF: —

Rarity: Common

This Spell Card destroys one face-up Trap Card on the Field. It cannot destroy face-down Trap Cards.

SDY-049 Castle Walls

Card Type: Trap

Monster Type: —

Attribute: Trap

Level: —

ATK: —

DEF: —

Rarity: Common

Similar to "Reinforcements," use this card on Monsters in Defense Position. Send back the damage!

SDY-050 Ultimate Offering

Card Type: Trap

Monster Type: —

Attribute: Trap

Level: —

ATK: —

DEF: —

Rarity: Common

As long as this card is face-up on the Field, you can freely Normal Summon or Set the Monster in your hand during your Main Phase or your opponent's Battle Phase.

Starter Deck Kaiba

SDK-001 Blue-Eyes White Dragon

Card Type: Normal Monster
Monster Type: Dragon
Attribute: Light
Level: 8
ATK: 3000
DEF: 2500
Rarity: Ultra Rare

Kaiba's favorite Monster is the most powerful Normal Monster Card. Destroying "Blue-Eyes" without a Spell Card will be difficult!

SDK-002 Hitotsu-Me Giant

Card Type: Normal Monster
Monster Type: Beast-Warrior
Attribute: Earth
Level: 4
ATK: 1200
DEF: 1000
Rarity: Common

Even Kaiba uses this Beast-Warrior-Type Monster. Be sure to put its high ATK to use!

SDK-003 Ryu-Kishin

Card Type: Normal Monster
Monster Type: Fiend
Attribute: Dark
Level: 3
ATK: 1000
DEF: 500
Rarity: Common

A mysterious new fiendish statue stands among ruins.... This must be "Ryu-Kishin"! Destroy it from afar!

SDK-004 The Wicked Worm Beast

Card Type: Effect Monster
Monster Type: Beast
Attribute: Earth
Level: 3
ATK: 1400
DEF: 700
Rarity: Common

If this Monster is destroyed during the Battle Phase, it will not return to your hand.

SDK-005 Battle Ox

Card Type: Normal Monster
Monster Type: Beast-Warrior
Attribute: Earth
Level: 4
ATK: 1700
DEF: 1000
Rarity: Common

This ox wears armor and wields a large axe, making it as strong as it looks. You don't need to offer another Monster for a Tribute to Summon "Battle Ox," making this Monster extremely useful.

SDK-006 Koumori Dragon

Card Type: Normal Monster
Monster Type: Dragon
Attribute: Dark
Level: 4
ATK: 1500
DEF: 1200
Rarity: Common

Even Yugi uses this black Dragon. It fires flames from its mouth and throws down enemies with its large tail. The souls of anyone who looks at this Monster becomes corrupted.

SDK-007 Judge Man

Card Type: Normal Monster
Monster Type: Warrior
Attribute: Earth
Level: 6
ATK: 2200
DEF: 1500
Rarity: Common

One of the most powerful Level 6 Monsters was also used in Kaiba's Deck.

SDK-008 Rogue Doll

Card Type: Normal Monster
Monster Type: Spellcaster
Attribute: Light
Level: 4
ATK: 1600
DEF: 1000
Rarity: Common

It has high ATK, but you can Summon this Monster without having to offer another Monster for a Tribute! However, its DEF is low.

SDK-009 Kojikocy

Card Type: Normal Monster
Monster Type: Warrior
Attribute: Earth
Level: 4
ATK: 1500
DEF: 1200
Rarity: Common

This Warrior has extremely powerful destructive powers! It will definitely be a core force in Warrior-Type Decks.

SDK-010 Uraby

Card Type:
Normal Monster

Monster Type:
Dinosaur

Attribute:
Earth

Level: 4

ATK: 1500

DEF: 800

Rarity:
Common

This powerful Dinosaur has overwhelming strength and will eat and swallow anyone it sets its sights on.

SDK-011 Gyakutenno Megami

Card Type:
Normal Monster

Monster Type:
Fairy

Attribute:
Light

Level: 6

ATK: 1800

DEF: 2000

Rarity:
Common

One of the strongest goddesses, "Gyakutenno Megami" has higher DEF than ATK.

SDK-012 Mystic Horseman

Card Type:
Normal Monster

Monster Type:
Beast

Attribute:
Earth

Level: 4

ATK: 1300

DEF: 1550

Rarity:
Common

A legendary half-man/half-horse creature, "Mystic Horseman" runs extremely fast, and its speedy attacks are truly horrifying.

SDK-013 Terra the Terrible

Card Type:
Normal Monster

Monster Type:
Fiend

Attribute:
Dark

Level: 4

ATK: 1200

DEF: 1300

Rarity:
Common

"Terra the Terrible" has average abilities, so you can entrust it with both attack and defense.

SDK-014 Dark Titan of Terror

Card Type:
Normal Monster

Monster Type:
Fiend

Attribute:
Dark

Level: 4

ATK: 1300

DEF: 1100

Rarity:
Common

This Monster enters your dreams and turns them into nightmares. He enjoys watching your horror.

SDK-015 Dark Assailant

Card Type:
Normal Monster

Monster Type:
Zombie

Attribute:
Dark

Level: 4

ATK: 1200

DEF: 1200

Rarity:
Common

Due to his popularity, he hasn't received any jobs recently.... It's hard to be famous.

SDK-016 Master & Expert

Card Type:
Normal Monster

Monster Type:
Beast

Attribute:
Earth

Level: 4

ATK: 1200

DEF: 1000

Rarity:
Common

The duo fight in perfect sync both offensively and defensively. However, their low ATK is their biggest weakness.

SDK-017 Unknown Warrior of Fiend

Card Type:
Normal Monster

Monster Type:
Warrior

Attribute:
Dark

Level: 3

ATK: 1000

DEF: 500

Rarity:
Common

"Unknown Warrior of Fiend" slices enemies by wielding a sword at supersonic speed. This is one of the fastest Warriors.

Card Catalog

SDK-018 Mystic Clown

Card Type:	Normal Monster
Monster Type:	Fiend
Attribute:	Dark
Level:	4
ATK:	1500
DEF:	1000
Rarity:	Common

Though not as powerful as "Rogue Doll," this low-level Monster has high ATK, making it a dangerous force!

SDK-019 Ogre of the Black Shadow

Card Type:	Normal Monster
Monster Type:	Beast-Warrior
Attribute:	Earth
Level:	4
ATK:	1200
DEF:	1400
Rarity:	Common

It can only move in straight lines, so you may think this Monster is easy to destroy. However, since it moves so fast, it evades many attacks.

SDK-020 Dark Energy

Card Type:	Spell
Monster Type:	—
Attribute:	Spell
Level:	—
ATK:	—
DEF:	—
Rarity:	Common

This energy source for Fiend-Type Monsters was created by compressing air from the underworld. Fiends use this energy to power-up!

SDK-021 Invigoration

Card Type:	Spell
Monster Type:	—
Attribute:	Spell
Level:	—
ATK:	—
DEF:	—
Rarity:	Common

This card affects many Warrior- and Plant-Type Monsters. Use this card with "Legendary Sword!"

SDK-022 Dark Hole

Card Type:	Spell
Monster Type:	—
Attribute:	Spell
Level:	—
ATK:	—
DEF:	—
Rarity:	Common

"Dark Hole" is very effective when the Duel is deadlocked against an opponent who is using Monsters with high DEF!

SDK-023 Ookazi

Card Type:	Spell
Monster Type:	—
Attribute:	Spell
Level:	—
ATK:	—
DEF:	—
Rarity:	Common

During meals, there's flames on the stove. If it turns into a fire.... Be careful to avoid disasters!

SDK-024 Ryu-Kishin Powered

Card Type:	Normal Monster
Monster Type:	Fiend
Attribute:	Dark
Level:	4
ATK:	1600
DEF:	1200
Rarity:	Common

Kaiba uses this beefed-up version of "Ryu-Kishin." Its armorlike body and huge sharp claws power up its abilities.

SDK-025 Swordstalker

Card Type:	Normal Monster
Monster Type:	Warrior
Attribute:	Dark
Level:	6
ATK:	2000
DEF:	1600
Rarity:	Common

"Swordstalker's" sword is said to be powered by the spirits of defeated Monsters.

TRADING CARD GAME

SDK-026 La Jinn the Mystical Genie of the Lamp

Card Type:
Normal Monster

Monster Type:
Fiend

Attribute:
Dark

Level: 4

ATK: 1800

DEF: 1000

Rarity:
Common

If you ask this Fiend for crazy wishes, he'll be upset....

SDK-027 Rude Kaiser

Card Type:
Normal Monster

Monster Type:
Beast-Warrior

Attribute:
Earth

Level: 5

ATK: 1800

DEF: 1600

Rarity:
Common

The huge axes connected to both arms can cleave a rock in a single slice. Beast-Warriors have high ATK, and "Rude Kaiser" is one of the strongest among them.

SDK-028 Destroyer Golem

Card Type:
Normal Monster

Monster Type:
Rock

Attribute:
Earth

Level: 4

ATK: 1500

DEF: 1000

Rarity:
Common

You can count on "Destroyer Golem's" high ATK in combat, but beware—its DEF is surprisingly low!

SDK-029 Skull Red Bird

Card Type:
Normal Monster

Monster Type:
Winged Beast

Attribute:
Wind

Level: 4

ATK: 1550

DEF: 1200

Rarity:
Common

"Skull Red Bird" is not as strong as "Rogue Doll," it's a decently powerful Winged Beast. Power it up with the Mountain Field Spell Card!

SDK-030 D. Human

Card Type:
Normal Monster

Monster Type:
Warrior

Attribute:
Earth

Level: 4

ATK: 1300

DEF: 1100

Rarity:
Common

"D. Human" wields a weapon created from a Dragon, so Dragons sometime attack him for vengeance!

SDK-031 Pale Beast

Card Type:
Normal Monster

Monster Type:
Beast

Attribute:
Earth

Level: 4

ATK: 1500

DEF: 1200

Rarity:
Common

Living deep in the shadows of a forest, the pair of eyes on "Pale Beast's" chin help it find prey.

SDK-032 Fissure

Card Type:
Spell

Monster Type: —

Attribute:
Spell

Level: —

ATK: —

DEF: —

Rarity:
Common

This card affects face-up Monster Cards. Even the mightiest Monster Cards cannot escape this effect!

SDK-033 Trap Hole

Card Type:
Trap

Monster Type: —

Attribute:
Trap

Level: —

ATK: —

DEF: —

Rarity:
Common

Activate "Trap Hole" when your opponent Normal Summons or Flip Summons a Monster!

Card Catalog

SDK-034 Two-Pronged Attack

Card Type: **Trap**
Monster Type: —
Attribute: **Trap**
Level: —
ATK: —
DEF: —
Rarity: **Common**

"Two-Pronged Attack" is very useful when you have many Monsters on your Field. Use it as soon as your opponent Summons a powerful Monster!

SDK-035 De-Spell

Card Type: **Spell**
Monster Type: —
Attribute: **Spell**
Level: —
ATK: —
DEF: —
Rarity: **Common**

This Spell Card can even destroy face-down Spell Cards. If the chosen face-down card is a Trap Card, then return the Trap Card back to normal.

SDK-036 Monster Reborn

Card Type: **Spell**
Monster Type: —
Attribute: **Spell**
Level: —
ATK: —
DEF: —
Rarity: **Common**

If there's a Monster Card in the Graveyard, use this Spell Card to resurrect it and make it part of your team! This is an extremely important card!

SDK-037 The Inexperienced Spy

Card Type: **Spell**
Monster Type: —
Attribute: **Spell**
Level: —
ATK: —
DEF: —
Rarity: **Common**

Since he's still in training, he can only see one card in your opponent's hand. Choose a card that looks suspicious.

SDK-038 Reinforcements

Card Type: **Trap**
Monster Type: —
Attribute: **Trap**
Level: —
ATK: —
DEF: —
Rarity: **Common**

Put a weak Monster in Attack Position, and use this Trap Card when your opponent attacks. It's a counterattack!

SDK-039 Ancient Telescope

Card Type: **Spell**
Monster Type: —
Attribute: **Spell**
Level: —
ATK: —
DEF: —
Rarity: **Common**

This very useful card lets you see your opponent's cards and prepare your strategy for the next five turns.

SDK-040 Just Desserts

Card Type: **Trap**
Monster Type: —
Attribute: **Trap**
Level: —
ATK: —
DEF: —
Rarity: **Common**

If your opponent has five Monsters on the Field, then you can deal 2500 points of damage, but this is easier said than done. It should be good to activate this Trap Card when your opponent has three Monster Cards on the Field.

SDK-041 Lord of D.

Card Type: **Effect Monster**
Monster Type: **Spellcaster**
Attribute: **Dark**
Level: **4**
ATK: **1200**
DEF: **1100**
Rarity: **Super Rare**

"Lord of D." can protect all Dragons, but that's not all! Using "Lord of D." with "The Flute of Summoning Dragon" forms a devastating combo!

SDK-042 The Flute of Summoning Dragon

Card Type: **Spell**
Monster Type: —
Attribute: **Spell**
Level: —
ATK: —
DEF: —
Rarity: **Super Rare**

You can Special Summon not one, but two "Blue-Eyes White Dragons" on the same turn! Your opponent will be dealt a crippling blow instantly. This card seems unfair....

SDK-043 Mysterious Puppeteer

Card Type:
Effect Monster

Monster Type:
Warrior

Attribute:
Earth

Level: 4

ATK: 1000

DEF: 1500

Rarity:
Common

This useful card allows you to regain Life Points even when your opponent Summons a Monster. Combo: When "Mysterious Puppeteer" is face-up on the Field, use "Ultimate Offering" and Summon your Monsters.

SDK-044 Trap Master

Card Type:
Effect Monster

Monster Type:
Warrior

Attribute:
Earth

Level: 3

ATK: 500

DEF: 1100

Rarity:
Common

You can destroy your opponent's Trap Card without it activating. It may be fun to Set this Monster on your first turn. It will baffle your opponent and throw his or her game off-track.

SDK-045 Sogen

Card Type:
Spell

Monster Type: —

Attribute:
Spell

Level: —

ATK: —

DEF: —

Rarity:
Common

This Spell Card transforms the Field into a scenic vast grassland. "Sogen" gives Warrior- and Beast-Warrior-Type Monster an advantage in battle!

SDK-046 Hane-Hane

Card Type:
Effect Monster

Monster Type:
Beast

Attribute:
Earth

Level: 2

ATK: 450

DEF: 500

Rarity:
Common

Even if face-down "Hane-Hane" is destroyed in battle, you return one Monster on the field, but please remember that you can not return "Hane-Hane" itself if it is destroyed.

SDK-047 Reverse Trap

Card Type:
Trap

Monster Type: —

Attribute:
Trap

Level: —

ATK: —

DEF: —

Rarity:
Common

This card counteracts all the Spell Cards and the like that are powering up Monsters. This is a scary Trap Card!

SDK-048 Remove Trap

Card Type:
Spell

Monster Type: —

Attribute:
Spell

Level: —

ATK: —

DEF: —

Rarity:
Common

This Spell Card destroys one face-up Trap Card on the Field. It cannot destroy face-down Trap Cards.

SDK-049 Castle Walls

Card Type:
Trap

Monster Type: —

Attribute:
Trap

Level: —

ATK: —

DEF: —

Rarity:
Common

Similar to "Reinforcements," use this card on Monsters in Defense Position. Send back the damage!

SDK-050 Ultimate Offering

Card Type:
Trap

Monster Type: —

Attribute:
Trap

Level: —

ATK: —

DEF: —

Rarity:
Common

As long as this card is face-up on the Field, you can freely Normal Summon or Set the Monster in your hand during your Main Phase or your opponent's Battle Phase.

Legend of Blue-Eyes White Dragon

LOB-001 Blue-Eyes White Dragon

Card Type: Normal Monster
Monster Type: Dragon
Attribute: Light
Level: 8
ATK: 3000
DEF: 2500
Rarity: Ultra Rare

Kaiba's favorite Monster is the most powerful Normal Monster Card. Destroying "Blue-Eyes" without a Spell Card will be difficult!

LOB-002 Hitotsu-Me Giant

Card Type: Normal Monster
Monster Type: Beast-Warrior
Attribute: Earth
Level: 4
ATK: 1200
DEF: 1000
Rarity: Common

Even Kaiba uses this Beast-Warrior-Type Monster. Be sure to put its high ATK to use!

LOB-003 Flame Swordsman

Card Type: Fusion Monster
Monster Type: Warrior
Attribute: Fire
Level: 5
ATK: 1800
DEF: 1600
Rarity: Super Rare

This expert swordsman wields a sword enveloped by flames. Joey uses "Flame Swordsman" as his trump card to get out of jams!

LOB-004 Skull Servant

Card Type: Normal Monster
Monster Type: Zombie
Attribute: Dark
Level: 1
ATK: 300
DEF: 200
Rarity: Common

Find one of these skeleton servants, and it feels as if thirty more are lurking behind. "Skull Servant" transforms into various things when fused.

LOB-005 Dark Magician

Card Type: Normal Monster
Monster Type: Spellcaster
Attribute: Dark
Level: 7
ATK: 2500
DEF: 2100
Rarity: Ultra Rare

A high-ranking magician of the Spellcaster-Type, the "Dark Magician" is very dangerous unless you destroy him as soon as your opponent places him on the Field.

LOB-006 Gaia The Fierce Knight

Card Type: Normal Monster
Monster Type: Warrior
Attribute: Earth
Level: 7
ATK: 2300
DEF: 2100
Rarity: Ultra Rare

Yugi uses this top-class Warrior. Don't fail to include this card in a Warrior-Type Deck!

LOB-007 Celtic Guardian

Card Type: Normal Monster
Monster Type: Warrior
Attribute: Earth
Level: 4
ATK: 1400
DEF: 1200
Rarity: Super Rare

With high ATK, "Celtic Guardian" is an elite Warrior. He slices his enemies with his skilled techniques!

LOB-008 Basic Insect

Card Type: Normal Monster
Monster Type: Insect
Attribute: Earth
Level: 2
ATK: 500
DEF: 700
Rarity: Common

This Insect is basically not very strong, but it likes to frolic in the Forest Field.

LOB-009 Mammoth Graveyard

Card Type: Normal Monster
Monster Type: Dinosaur
Attribute: Earth
Level: 3
ATK: 1200
DEF: 800
Rarity: Common

Even Yugi uses this Dinosaur-Type Card. It has balanced ATK!

TRADING CARD GAME

LOB-010 Silver Fang

Card Type:
Normal Monster

Monster Type:
Beast

Attribute:
Earth

Level: 3

ATK: 1200

DEF: 800

Rarity:
Common

Yugi often uses this feral wolf in Duels. Power it up and defeat your opponent!

LOB-011 Dark Gray

Card Type:
Normal Monster

Monster Type:
Beast

Attribute:
Earth

Level: 3

ATK: 800

DEF: 900

Rarity:
Common

This rare creature's ATK and DEF are well-balanced. If you ever get a chance to see "Dark Gray," you're extremely lucky!

LOB-012 Trial of Nightmare

Card Type:
Normal Monster

Monster Type:
Fiend

Attribute:
Dark

Level: 4

ATK: 1300

DEF: 900

Rarity:
Common

This mid-level Monster has high ATK.

LOB-013 Nemuriko

Card Type:
Normal Monster

Monster Type:
Spellcaster

Attribute:
Dark

Level: 3

ATK: 800

DEF: 700

Rarity:
Common

"Nemuriko" is a Spellcaster that lures people into eternal sleep! Whether "Nemuriko" is a girl or a boy remains a mystery.

LOB-014 The 13th Grave

Card Type:
Normal Monster

Monster Type:
Zombie

Attribute:
Dark

Level: 3

ATK: 1200

DEF: 900

Rarity:
Common

This Zombie appeared from grave #13—which was supposedly empty!

LOB-015 Charubin the Fire Knight

Card Type:
Fusion Monster

Monster Type:
Pyro

Attribute:
Fire

Level: 3

ATK: 1100

DEF: 800

Rarity:
Rare

Using the Spell Card "Polymerization," this Warrior comes to life when an egg is cooked at high temperature. Beware of its spiked mace!

LOB-016 Flame Manipulator

Card Type:
Normal Monster

Monster Type:
Spellcaster

Attribute:
Fire

Level: 3

ATK: 900

DEF: 1000

Rarity:
Common

When fused, this Spellcaster transforms into "Flame Swordsman." He's better at defending than he is at attacking!

LOB-017 Monster Egg

Card Type:
Normal Monster

Monster Type:
Warrior

Attribute:
Earth

Level: 3

ATK: 600

DEF: 900

Rarity:
Common

The creature spends most of its time hiding inside an egg, but it is still quite a Warrior. It usually doesn't attack and keeps defending.

LOB-018 Firegrass

Card Type:
Normal Monster

Monster Type:
Plant

Attribute:
Earth

Level: 2

ATK: 700

DEF: 600

Rarity:
Common

Use this Fusion-Material Monster to Summon the Fusion Monster "Darkfire Dragon!" Alone, it will struggle in battle.

Card Catalog

LOB-019 Darkfire Dragon

Card Type: Fusion Monster
Monster Type: Dragon
Attribute: Dark
Level: 4
ATK: 1500
DEF: 1250
Rarity: Rare

"Petit Dragon" has wrapped itself in flames and evolved to "Darkfire Dragon." This Fusion Monster has higher ATK than before.

LOB-020 Dark King of the Abyss

Card Type: Normal Monster
Monster Type: Fiend
Attribute: Dark
Level: 3
ATK: 1200
DEF: 800
Rarity: Common

"Dark King of the Abyss" is a Zombie-Type Monster with DARK.

LOB-021 Fiend Reflection #2

Card Type: Normal Monster
Monster Type: Winged Beast
Attribute: Light
Level: 4
ATK: 1100
DEF: 1400
Rarity: Common

This Winged Beast flies around at high speed, so it takes steady aim to nail it. Destroy it before it starts calling out for its friends!

LOB-022 Fusionist

Card Type: Fusion Monster
Monster Type: Beast
Attribute: Earth
Level: 3
ATK: 900
DEF: 700
Rarity: Rare

This is a Fusion Monster, but it is not very useful. However, cat lovers will find it irresistible.

LOB-023 Turtle Tiger

Card Type: Normal Monster
Monster Type: Aqua
Attribute: Water
Level: 4
ATK: 1000
DEF: 1500
Rarity: Common

"Turtle Tiger's" high DEF allows it to take attacks head-on!

LOB-024 Petit Dragon

Card Type: Normal Monster
Monster Type: Dragon
Attribute: Wind
Level: 2
ATK: 600
DEF: 700
Rarity: Common

During battles, "Petit Dragon" attacks using its entire body in a crazy manner. Is this a special unique dragon fighting style?

LOB-025 Petit Angel

Card Type: Normal Monster
Monster Type: Fairy
Attribute: Light
Level: 3
ATK: 600
DEF: 900
Rarity: Common

This tiny young angel is very speedy! Because ATK is very low, Set in Defense Position.

LOB-026 Hinotama Soul

Card Type: Normal Monster
Monster Type: Pyro
Attribute: Fire
Level: 2
ATK: 600
DEF: 500
Rarity: Common

You'll be toast if this blazing sentient flame crashes into you!

LOB-027 Aqua Madoor

Card Type: Normal Monster
Monster Type: Spellcaster
Attribute: Water
Level: 4
ATK: 1200
DEF: 2000
Rarity: Rare

"Aqua Madoor" has high DEF, and its ATK is not bad either!

LOB-028 Kagemusha of the Blue Flame

Card Type:
Normal Monster

Monster Type:
Warrior

Attribute:
Earth

Level: 2

ATK: 800

DEF: 400

Rarity:
Common

This Warrior's ATK is twice as high as his DEF. Therefore, you may want to use it in Attack Position instead of Defense Position.

LOB-029 Flame Ghost

Card Type:
Fusion Monster

Monster Type:
Zombie

Attribute:
Dark

Level: 3

ATK: 1000

DEF: 800

Rarity:
Rare

Created when "Dissolverock" walks above a sleeping "Skull Servant," "Flame Ghost" is hot to the touch!

LOB-030 Two-Mouth Darkruler

Card Type:
Normal Monster

Monster Type:
Dinosaur

Attribute:
Earth

Level: 3

ATK: 900

DEF: 700

Rarity:
Common

A rare Dinosaur with two mouths, "Two-Mouth Darkruler's" electric attack is powerful but not unbearable!

LOB-031 Dissolverock

Card Type:
Normal Monster

Monster Type:
Rock

Attribute:
Earth

Level: 3

ATK: 900

DEF: 1000

Rarity:
Common

This magma Monster moves around everywhere! If it suddenly starts getting hot around you, you know "Dissolverock" has come to pay you a visit.

LOB-032 Root Water

Card Type:
Normal Monster

Monster Type:
Fish

Attribute:
Water

Level: 3

ATK: 900

DEF: 800

Rarity:
Common

"Root Water" attacks from the depths of the sea by creating large tsunamis. You should fight on land to avoid drowning!

LOB-033 The Furious Sea King

Card Type:
Normal Monster

Monster Type:
Aqua

Attribute:
Water

Level: 3

ATK: 800

DEF: 700

Rarity:
Common

Offer this mid-ranking Aqua-Type Monster as a Tribute to Summon high-level Monster Cards.

LOB-034 Green Phantom King

Card Type:
Normal Monster

Monster Type:
Plant

Attribute:
Earth

Level: 3

ATK: 500

DEF: 1600

Rarity:
Common

This king of plants values all life, so it prefers combat when it's protecting its friends instead of attacking to hurt its enemy.

LOB-035 Ray & Temperature

Card Type:
Normal Monster

Monster Type:
Fairy

Attribute:
Light

Level: 3

ATK: 1000

DEF: 1000

Rarity:
Common

This Fairy specializes in combo attacks! The sun emits thermal rays while the north wind slices through the enemy with its mighty gale!

LOB-036 King Fog

Card Type:
Normal Monster

Monster Type:
Fiend

Attribute:
Dark

Level: 3

ATK: 1000

DEF: 900

Rarity:
Common

This Fiend ambushes the enemy by hiding in smoke. Before you know it, a thick smoke surrounds and blinds you.

LOB-037 Mystical Sheep #2

Card Type: Normal Monster

Monster Type: Beast

Attribute: Earth

Level: 3

ATK: 800

DEF: 1000

Rarity: Common

This scary Beast will hypnotize you with its long tail. It boasts large horns and a warm-looking coat.

LOB-038 Masaki the Legendary Swordsman

Card Type: Normal Monster

Monster Type: Warrior

Attribute: Earth

Level: 4

ATK: 1100

DEF: 1100

Rarity: Common

The legendary Warrior has revived in present times. Dressed in the same armor during battle, he strikes his enemy with his favorite sword.

LOB-039 Kurama

Card Type: Normal Monster

Monster Type: Winged Beast

Attribute: Wind

Level: 3

ATK: 800

DEF: 800

Rarity: Common

Kurama's ATK and DEF are exactly the same. Set this Monster in Defense Position until you can Summon a stronger Monster.

LOB-040 Legendary Sword

Card Type: Spell

Monster Type: —

Attribute: Spell

Level: —

ATK: —

DEF: —

Rarity: Common

"Legendary Sword" powers up Warrior-Type Monsters, regardless of their Attribute. It's reassuring to have at least one in your Deck.

LOB-041 Beast Fangs

Card Type: Spell

Monster Type: —

Attribute: Spell

Level: —

ATK: —

DEF: —

Rarity: Common

Overall, Beast-Type Monsters have high DEF, and "Beast Fangs" will strengthen your defense even greater.

LOB-042 Violet Crystal

Card Type: Spell

Monster Type: —

Attribute: Spell

Level: —

ATK: —

DEF: —

Rarity: Common

Use "Violet Crystal" to power up your Zombie-Type Monster and destroy your opponent's Monsters.

LOB-043 Book of Secret Arts

Card Type: Spell

Monster Type: —

Attribute: Spell

Level: —

ATK: —

DEF: —

Rarity: Common

Use this book on "Dark Magician" to easily destroy every Monster Card, except "Blue-Eyes White Dragon!"

LOB-044 Power of Kaishin

Card Type: Spell

Monster Type: —

Attribute: Spell

Level: —

ATK: —

DEF: —

Rarity: Common

Use "Power of Kaishin" to power up Aqua-Type Monsters.

LOB-045 Dragon Capture Jar

Card Type: Trap

Monster Type: —

Attribute: Trap

Level: —

ATK: —

DEF: —

Rarity: Rare

Dragon-Types should be wary of this Trap Card. Even the "Stop Defense" Spell Card can't affect "Dragon Capture Jar!"

LOB-046 Forest

Card Type: Spell

Monster Type: —

Attribute: Spell

Level: —

ATK: —

DEF: —

Rarity: Common

This valuable Spell Card creates a deep forest that aids Insect, Plant, Beast, and Beast-Warrior-Types in battles.

LOB-047 Wasteland

Card Type: Spell

Monster Type: —

Attribute: Spell

Level: —

ATK: —

DEF: —

Rarity: Common

"Wasteland" transforms the Field into a desolate withered wasteland. This card powers up Dinosaur, Zombie, and Rock-Types!

LOB-048 Mountain

Card Type: Spell

Monster Type: —

Attribute: Spell

Level: —

ATK: —

DEF: —

Rarity: Common

This Spell Card creates terrain that helps Dragon, Winged Beast, and Thunder-Types. If you power up "Blue-Eyes White Dragon," it will be invincible!

LOB-049 Sogen

Card Type: Spell

Monster Type: —

Attribute: Spell

Level: —

ATK: —

DEF: —

Rarity: Common

This Spell Card transforms the Field into a scenic vast grassland. "Sogen" gives Warrior and Beast-Warrior-Types an advantage in battle!

LOB-050 Umi

Card Type: Spell

Monster Type: —

Attribute: Spell

Level: —

ATK: —

DEF: —

Rarity: Common

This terrain allows Sea Serpent, Fish, Thunder, and Aqua-Types to swim freely! On the other hand, Machine and Pyro-Types are weakened.

LOB-051 Yami

Card Type: Spell

Monster Type: —

Attribute: Spell

Level: —

ATK: —

DEF: —

Rarity: Common

Since Fairy-Type Monsters crave the light, they're weak in Yami terrain. However, this terrain strengthens Fiend and Spellcaster-Types who thrive on magical powers!

LOB-052 Dark Hole

Card Type: Spell

Monster Type: —

Attribute: Spell

Level: —

ATK: —

DEF: —

Rarity: Super Rare

"Dark Hole" is very effective when the Duel is deadlocked against an opponent who is using Monsters with high DEF!

LOB-053 Raigeki

Card Type: Spell

Monster Type: —

Attribute: Spell

Level: —

ATK: —

DEF: —

Rarity: Super Rare

This must-have card destroys all your opponent's Monsters. No Monster Card can withstand its powerful destructive force!

LOB-054 Red Medicine

Card Type: Spell

Monster Type: —

Attribute: Spell

Level: —

ATK: —

DEF: —

Rarity: Common

This bubbling red liquid will refill 500 Life Points, but I wonder how it tastes....

LOB-055 Sparks

Card Type: Spell
Monster Type: —
Attribute: Spell
Level: —
ATK: —
DEF: —
Rarity: Common

This hot little magical flame is not that useful, but it can still be annoying when used against you.

LOB-056 Hinotama

Card Type: Spell
Monster Type: —
Attribute: Spell
Level: —
ATK: —
DEF: —
Rarity: Common

"Hinotama" deals 500 points of damage to your opponent's Life Points by hurling fireballs at your opponent. These fireballs aren't very powerful, but they can sometimes cause fires.

LOB-057 Fissure

Card Type: Spell
Monster Type: —
Attribute: Spell
Level: —
ATK: —
DEF: —
Rarity: Rare

This card affects face-up Monster Cards. Even the mightiest Monster Cards cannot escape this effect!

LOB-058 Trap Hole

Card Type: Trap
Monster Type: —
Attribute: Trap
Level: —
ATK: —
DEF: —
Rarity: Super Rare

Activate "Trap Hole" when your opponent Flip Summons a Monster Card face-up or Summons a Monster face-up directly!

LOB-059 Polymerization

Card Type: Spell
Monster Type: —
Attribute: Spell
Level: —
ATK: —
DEF: —
Rarity: Super Rare

This Spell Card combines various Monsters to transform them into a new and powerful Monster Card. This increases your chances for victory!

LOB-060 Remove Trap

Card Type: Spell
Monster Type: —
Attribute: Spell
Level: —
ATK: —
DEF: —
Rarity: Common

This Spell Card destroys one face-up Trap Card on the Field. It cannot destroy face-down Trap Cards.

LOB-061 Two-Pronged Attack

Card Type: Trap
Monster Type: —
Attribute: Trap
Level: —
ATK: —
DEF: —
Rarity: Rare

"Two-Pronged Attack" is very useful when you have many Monsters on your Field. Use it as soon as your opponent Normal Summons or Flip Summons a powerful Monster!

LOB-062 Mystical Elf

Card Type: Normal Monster
Monster Type: Spellcaster
Attribute: Light
Level: 4
ATK: 800
DEF: 2000
Rarity: Super Rare

Rely on "Mystical Elf" for defense. However, since she has low ATK, she's easy prey for "Fissure...."

LOB-063 Tyhone

Card Type: Normal Monster
Monster Type: Winged Beast
Attribute: Wind
Level: 4
ATK: 1200
DEF: 1400
Rarity: Common

"Tyhone" launches long-range attacks from the mountains, so look out above when you enter the mountains!

LOB-064 Beaver Warrior

Card Type: Normal Monster
Monster Type: Beast-Warrior
Attribute: Earth
Level: 4
ATK: 1200
DEF: 1500
Rarity: Common

"Beaver Warrior" is one of Yugi's favorite Beast-Warriors. Set this Monster first in Defense Position, then switch it to Attack Position when you see an opening!

LOB-065 Gravedigger Ghoul

Card Type: Spell
Monster Type: —
Attribute: Spell
Level: —
ATK: —
DEF: —
Rarity: Rare

Use this card as a countermeasure against "Monster Reborn." However, you won't be able to resurrect the Monsters with your "Monster Reborn" either, so use "Gravedigger Ghoul" wisely.

LOB-066 Curse of Dragon

Card Type: Normal Monster
Monster Type: Dragon
Attribute: Dark
Level: 5
ATK: 2000
DEF: 1500
Rarity: Super Rare

This cursed Dragon chars everything with its breath of flame. Instead of Setting it in Defense Position, attack!

LOB-067 Karbonala Warrior

Card Type: Fusion Monster
Monster Type: Warrior
Attribute: Earth
Level: 4
ATK: 1500
DEF: 1200
Rarity: Rare

"Karbonala Warrior" is created when the close-knit "M-Warrior" brothers fuse. However, "Karbonala Warrior's" personality is quite different than before.

LOB-068 Giant Soldier of Stone

Card Type: Normal Monster
Monster Type: Rock
Attribute: Earth
Level: 3
ATK: 1300
DEF: 2000
Rarity: Rare

This card will be the main Monster in a Rock-Type Deck. For a Level 3 Monster, the ATK and DEF are amazing!

LOB-069 Uraby

Card Type: Normal Monster
Monster Type: Dinosaur
Attribute: Earth
Level: 4
ATK: 1500
DEF: 800
Rarity: Common

This powerful Dinosaur has overwhelming strength and will eat and swallow anyone it sets its sights on.

LOB-070 Red-Eyes B. Dragon

Card Type: Normal Monster
Monster Type: Dragon
Attribute: Dark
Level: 7
ATK: 2400
DEF: 2000
Rarity: Ultra Rare

Joey received this rare card by defeating Rex Raptor. This Monster can become even stronger if it fused with another Monster by "Polymerization!"

LOB-071 Reaper of the Cards

Card Type: Effect Monster
Monster Type: Fiend
Attribute: Dark
Level: 5
ATK: 1380
DEF: 1930
Rarity: Rare

After destroying a Trap Card on the Field, "Reaper of the Cards" can provide strong defense. However, you must offer another Monster as a Tribute to Set "Reaper of the Cards."

LOB-072 Witty Phantom

Card Type: Normal Monster
Monster Type: Fiend
Attribute: Dark
Level: 4
ATK: 1400
DEF: 1300
Rarity: Common

This Fiend is a hard-working nice guy and is quite popular with the ladies of the underworld.

Card Catalog

LOB-073 Larvas

Card Type:
Normal Monster

Monster Type:
Beast

Attribute:
Earth

Level: 3

ATK: 800

DEF: 1000

Rarity:
Common

Although this peculiar creature is a bird, it sides with other Beasts. However, it's so weak.

LOB-074 Hard Armor

Card Type:
Normal Monster

Monster Type:
Warrior

Attribute:
Earth

Level: 3

ATK: 300

DEF: 1200

Rarity:
Common

Similar to "Armaill," this Warrior's specialty is defense. Does it have low ATK because it's only armor?

LOB-075 Man Eater

Card Type:
Normal Monster

Monster Type:
Plant

Attribute:
Earth

Level: 2

ATK: 800

DEF: 600

Rarity:
Common

This Plant-Type Monster has a scary face in the middle of its petals. However, it's not very strong....

LOB-076 M-Warrior #1

Card Type:
Normal Monster

Monster Type:
Warrior

Attribute:
Earth

Level: 3

ATK: 1000

DEF: 500

Rarity:
Common

"M-Warrior #1" launches combo attacks with "M-Warrior #2." Its specialty is offense.

LOB-077 M-Warrior #2

Card Type:
Normal Monster

Monster Type:
Warrior

Attribute:
Earth

Level: 3

ATK: 500

DEF: 1000

Rarity:
Common

When fused with "M-Warrior #1," this Warrior transforms to "Karbonala Warrior." "M-Warrior #2's" specialty is defense.

LOB-078 Spirit of the Harp

Card Type:
Normal Monster

Monster Type:
Fairy

Attribute:
Light

Level: 4

ATK: 800

DEF: 2000

Rarity:
Rare

This female Monster has very high DEF. If you use Yami Field Spell Card, "Spirit of the Harp" will power down.

LOB-079 Armaill

Card Type:
Normal Monster

Monster Type:
Warrior

Attribute:
Earth

Level: 3

ATK: 700

DEF: 1300

Rarity:
Common

This Warrior has higher DEF than ATK because it wields its three swords expertly when defending.

LOB-080 Terra the Terrible

Card Type:
Normal Monster

Monster Type:
Fiend

Attribute:
Dark

Level: 4

ATK: 1200

DEF: 1300

Rarity:
Common

"Terra the Terrible" has average abilities, so you can entrust it with both attack and defense.

LOB-081 Frenzied Panda

Card Type:
Normal Monster

Monster Type:
Beast

Attribute:
Earth

Level: 4

ATK: 1200

DEF: 1000

Rarity:
Common

"Frenzied Panda" prefers to eat meat than bamboo leaves. It hunts its prey with a bamboo spear.

LOB-082 Kumootoko

Card Type:
Normal Monster

Monster Type:
Insect

Attribute:
Earth

Level: 3

ATK: 700

DEF: 1400

Rarity:
Common

This Insect can move quickly in its web, so it's difficult to strike it!

LOB-083 Meda Bat

Card Type:
Normal Monster

Monster Type:
Fiend

Attribute:
Dark

Level: 2

ATK: 800

DEF: 400

Rarity:
Common

"Meda Bat" is an expert at attacking enemies, but it is horrible at defense. If it stares at you with its huge eye, you will definitely be startled.

LOB-084 Enchanting Mermaid

Card Type:
Normal Monster

Monster Type:
Fish

Attribute:
Water

Level: 3

ATK: 1200

DEF: 900

Rarity:
Common

This mermaid is as brutal as she is beautiful. She possesses high ATK, so don't be led astray!

LOB-085 Fireyarou

Card Type:
Normal Monster

Monster Type:
Pyro

Attribute:
Fire

Level: 4

ATK: 1300

DEF: 1000

Rarity:
Common

"Fireyarou" is one of the few Pyro-Type Monsters. He trains throughout the day to increase his own abilities. He's a hard worker!

LOB-086 Dragoness the Wicked Knight

Card Type:
Fusion Monster

Monster Type:
Warrior

Attribute:
Wind

Level: 3

ATK: 1200

DEF: 900

Rarity:
Rare

"Dragoness the Wicked Knight" looks really cool, but this Warrior's ATK and DEF are mediocre. Its favorite hobby is flying.

LOB-087 One-Eyed Shield Dragon

Card Type:
Normal Monster

Monster Type:
Dragon

Attribute:
Wind

Level: 3

ATK: 700

DEF: 1300

Rarity:
Common

This Dragon has high defense because it carries a shield. It flies to and fro and strikes when you're not ready.

LOB-088 Dark Energy

Card Type:
Spell

Monster Type: —

Attribute:
Spell

Level: —

ATK: —

DEF: —

Rarity:
Common

This energy source for Fiend-Type Monsters was created by compressing air from the underworld. Fiends use this energy to power up!

LOB-089 Laser Cannon Armor

Card Type:
Spell

Monster Type: —

Attribute:
Spell

Level: —

ATK: —

DEF: —

Rarity:
Common

This armor has been specially sized for Insects. Equip this card on your Insects to increase their ATK and DEF!

LOB-090 Vile Germs

Card Type:
Spell

Monster Type: —

Attribute:
Spell

Level: —

ATK: —

DEF: —

Rarity:
Common

Use "Vile Germs" to increase the power of your Plant-Type Monsters.

Card Catalog

LOB-091 Silver Bow and Arrow

Card Type: **Spell**
Monster Type: —
Attribute: **Spell**
Level: —
ATK: —
DEF: —
Rarity: **Common**

Only Fairies can equip this blessed bow and arrow to destroy evil creatures.

LOB-092 Dragon Treasure

Card Type: **Spell**
Monster Type: —
Attribute: **Spell**
Level: —
ATK: —
DEF: —
Rarity: **Common**

Dragons are already powerful to begin with, but this card powers them up even more. This card seems to have no weaknesses!

LOB-093 Electro-Whip

Card Type: **Spell**
Monster Type: —
Attribute: **Spell**
Level: —
ATK: —
DEF: —
Rarity: **Common**

This whip enhances the electricity generated from Thunder-Type Monsters. Use this card when the situation calls for it.

LOB-094 Mystical Moon

Card Type: **Spell**
Monster Type: —
Attribute: **Spell**
Level: —
ATK: —
DEF: —
Rarity: **Common**

You can strengthen Beast-Warrior-Type Monsters with "Mystical Moon." Include only as many "Mystical Moons" as you need in your Deck.

LOB-095 Stop Defense

Card Type: **Spell**
Monster Type: —
Attribute: **Spell**
Level: —
ATK: —
DEF: —
Rarity: **Rare**

Use "Stop Defense" on Monsters that have high DEF that are in Defense Position. Force it to switch to Attack Position.

LOB-096 Machine Conversion Factory

Card Type: **Spell**
Monster Type: —
Attribute: **Spell**
Level: —
ATK: —
DEF: —
Rarity: **Common**

This Spell Card drastically increases a Machine's powers. Rusted joints can now flex smoothly!

LOB-097 Raise Body Heat

Card Type: **Spell**
Monster Type: —
Attribute: **Spell**
Level: —
ATK: —
DEF: —
Rarity: **Common**

This gift will warm up your cold-blooded Dinosaur, allowing it focus on the Duel at hand.

LOB-098 Follow Wind

Card Type: **Spell**
Monster Type: —
Attribute: **Spell**
Level: —
ATK: —
DEF: —
Rarity: **Common**

These divine wings allow Winged Beasts to fly at top speed. Use it to increase their power.

LOB-099 Goblin's Secret Remedy

Card Type: **Spell**
Monster Type: —
Attribute: **Spell**
Level: —
ATK: —
DEF: —
Rarity: **Rare**

After you bite into this secret remedy cherished by goblin fairies, the bitterness will spread throughout your mouth.

LOB-100 Final Flame

Card Type:
Spell

Monster Type: —

Attribute:
Spell

Level: —

ATK: —

DEF: —

Rarity:
Rare

This glowing card does a whopping 600 points of damage to your opponent's Life Points! Save it for the final stroke.

LOB-101 Swords of Revealing Light

Card Type:
Spell

Monster Type: —

Attribute:
Spell

Level: —

ATK: —

DEF: —

Rarity:
Super Rare

This is an extremely powerful Spell Card. However, since this card stays on the Field for three turns, it can be destroyed by "De-Spell" or "Heavy Storm."

LOB-102 Metal Dragon

Card Type:
Fusion Monster

Monster Type:
Machine

Attribute:
Wind

Level: 6

ATK: 1850

DEF: 1700

Rarity:
Rare

This fusion requires "Steel Ogre Grotto #1," which is not an easy Monster to Summon. Therefore, use "Polymerization" while the card is in your hand.

LOB-103 Spike Seadra

Card Type:
Normal Monster

Monster Type:
Sea Serpent

Attribute:
Water

Level: 5

ATK: 1600

DEF: 1300

Rarity:
Common

"Spike Seadra" lives underwater, but it specializes in electric attacks because its skin is insulated.

LOB-104 Tripwire Beast

Card Type:
Normal Monster

Monster Type:
Thunder

Attribute:
Earth

Level: 4

ATK: 1200

DEF: 1300

Rarity:
Common

Stepping on "Tripwire Beast" won't cause it to explode, but it will unleash blasts of lightning!

LOB-105 Skull Red Bird

Card Type:
Normal Monster

Monster Type:
Winged Beast

Attribute:
Wind

Level: 4

ATK: 1550

DEF: 1200

Rarity:
Common

"Skull Red Bird" is not as strong as "Rogue Doll," it's a decently powerful Winged Beast. Power it up with the Mountain Field Spell Card!

LOB-106 Armed Ninja

Card Type:
Effect Monster

Monster Type:
Warrior

Attribute:
Earth

Level: 1

ATK: 300

DEF: 300

Rarity:
Rare

Use "Armed Ninja" when you do not have enough "De-Spell" cards in your Deck. It's surprisingly useful for a low-level card.

LOB-107 Flower Wolf

Card Type:
Fusion Monster

Monster Type:
Beast

Attribute:
Earth

Level: 5

ATK: 1800

DEF: 1400

Rarity:
Rare

This Fusion-Type Monster is relatively easy to Summon and has good ATK, so make it part of your normal Summoning strategy.

LOB-108 Man-Eater Bug

Card Type:
Effect Monster

Monster Type:
Insect

Attribute:
Earth

Level: 2

ATK: 450

DEF: 600

Rarity:
Super Rare

If "Man-Eater Bug" is the only Monster on the Field, its effect will destroy the "Man-Eater Bug" itself....

Card Catalog

LOB-109 Sand Stone

Card Type: Normal Monster
Monster Type: Rock
Attribute: Earth
Level: 5
ATK: 1300
DEF: 1600
Rarity: Common

Though "Sand Stone" is a high-level Rock-Type Monster, since its defenses are lower than "Giant Soldier of Stone," this card is difficult to use.

LOB-110 Hane-Hane

Card Type: Effect Monster
Monster Type: Beast
Attribute: Earth
Level: 2
ATK: 450
DEF: 500
Rarity: Rare

Even if face-down "Hane-Hane" is destroyed in battle, you return one Monster on the Field, but please remember that you can not return "Hane-Hane" itself if it is destroyed.

LOB-111 Misairuzame

Card Type: Normal Monster
Monster Type: Fish
Attribute: Water
Level: 5
ATK: 1400
DEF: 1600
Rarity: Common

If you befriend this extremely intelligent Fish, it will bring you many delicacies from the ocean.

LOB-112 Steel Ogre Grotto #1

Card Type: Normal Monster
Monster Type: Machine
Attribute: Earth
Level: 5
ATK: 1400
DEF: 1800
Rarity: Common

"Steel Ogre Grotto #1" is a high-level Machine-Type Monster, but even if you Summon it, it seems only to be good for defense....

LOB-113 Lesser Dragon

Card Type: Normal Monster
Monster Type: Dragon
Attribute: Wind
Level: 4
ATK: 1200
DEF: 1000
Rarity: Common

Use this low-level Monster as a Tribute to Summon other, more powerful Dragons.

LOB-114 Darkworld Thorns

Card Type: Normal Monster
Monster Type: Plant
Attribute: Earth
Level: 3
ATK: 1200
DEF: 900
Rarity: Common

This rose won't attack you unless you get too close. When it rains, it sways its body happily.

LOB-115 Drooling Lizard

Card Type: Normal Monster
Monster Type: Reptile
Attribute: Earth
Level: 3
ATK: 900
DEF: 800
Rarity: Common

There are very few Reptile-Type Monsters, and "Drooling Lizard" is one of them. This card may not be very useful.

LOB-116 Armored Starfish

Card Type: Normal Monster
Monster Type: Aqua
Attribute: Water
Level: 4
ATK: 850
DEF: 1400
Rarity: Common

A large starfish with a strong hide, "Armored Starfish's" high DEF makes it useful for strengthening your defense.

LOB-117 Succubus Knight

Card Type: Normal Monster
Monster Type: Warrior
Attribute: Dark
Level: 5
ATK: 1650
DEF: 1300
Rarity: Common

This extremely beautiful female Warrior can be further powered up by "Sword of Dark Destruction" because it has DARK.

LOB-118 Monster Reborn

Card Type:
Spell

Monster Type: —

Attribute:
Spell

Level: —

ATK: —

DEF: —

Rarity:
Ultra Rare

If there's a Monster Card in the Graveyard, use this Spell Card to resurrect it and make it part of your team! This is an extremely important card!

LOB-119 Pot of Greed

Card Type:
Spell

Monster Type: —

Attribute:
Spell

Level: —

ATK: —

DEF: —

Rarity:
Rare

This card is essential when you want to increase the cards in your hand or thin out your Deck.

LOB-120 Right Leg of the Forbidden One

Card Type:
Normal Monster

Monster Type:
Spellcaster

Attribute:
Dark

Level: 1

ATK: 200

DEF: 300

Rarity:
Ultra Rare

If at anytime you have five parts of Exodia, you win automatically!

LOB-121 Left Leg of the Forbidden One

Card Type:
Normal Monster

Monster Type:
Spellcaster

Attribute:
Dark

Level: 1

ATK: 200

DEF: 300

Rarity:
Ultra Rare

If at anytime you have five parts of Exodia, you win automatically!

LOB-122 Right Arm of the Forbidden One

Card Type:
Normal Monster

Monster Type:
Spellcaster

Attribute:
Dark

Level: 1

ATK: 200

DEF: 300

Rarity:
Ultra Rare

If at anytime you have five parts of Exodia, you win automatically!

LOB-123 Left Arm of the Forbidden One

Card Type:
Normal Monster

Monster Type:
Spellcaster

Attribute:
Dark

Level: 1

ATK: 200

DEF: 300

Rarity:
Ultra Rare

If at anytime you have five parts of Exodia, you win automatically!

LOB-124 Exodia the Forbidden One

Card Type:
Effect Monster

Monster Type:
Spellcaster

Attribute:
Dark

Level: 3

ATK: 1000

DEF: 1000

Rarity:
Ultra Rare

This is one of the five parts necessary to resurrect "Exodia the Forbidden One."

LOB-125 Gaia the Dragon Champion

Card Type:
Fusion Monster

Monster Type:
Dragon

Attribute:
Wind

Level: 7

ATK: 2600

DEF: 2100

Rarity:
Secret Rare

It is very difficult to acquire this Secret Rare Card. However, its strength is worth the struggle!

LOB-000 Tri-Horned Dragon

Card Type:
Normal Monster

Monster Type:
Dragon

Attribute:
Dark

Level: 8

ATK: 2850

DEF: 2350

Rarity:
Secret Rare

This Dragon is one of the most powerful Monsters in existence!

Metal Raiders

MRD-001 Feral Imp

Card Type: Normal Monster
Monster Type: Fiend
Attribute: Dark
Level: 4
ATK: 1300
DEF: 1400
Rarity: Common

This small Fiend's entire body is colored green. Its love of practical jokes makes it troublesome to deal with.

MRD-002 Winged Dragon, Guardian of the Fortress #1

Card Type: Normal Monster
Monster Type: Dragon
Attribute: Wind
Level: 4
ATK: 1400
DEF: 1200
Rarity: Common

Mountain battles are this Dragon's specialty. It frustrates enemies with sneak attacks!

MRD-003 Summoned Skull

Card Type: Normal Monster
Monster Type: Fiend
Attribute: Dark
Level: 6
ATK: 2500
DEF: 1200
Rarity: Ultra Rare

Though "Summoned Skull" is a high-level Fiend, it's easy to Summon and extremely useful.

MRD-004 Rock Ogre Grotto #1

Card Type: Normal Monster
Monster Type: Rock
Attribute: Earth
Level: 3
ATK: 800
DEF: 1200
Rarity: Common

Notice that "Rock Ogre Grotto #1's" ATK is lower than its DEF. Other Rock-Type Monsters may be better suited to your needs.

MRD-005 Armored Lizard

Card Type: Normal Monster
Monster Type: Reptile
Attribute: Earth
Level: 4
ATK: 1500
DEF: 1200
Rarity: Common

The main offensive card of the Reptile-Type Monsters, "Armored Lizard's" strength is that it is good to go in any terrain!

MRD-006 Killer Needle

Card Type: Normal Monster
Monster Type: Insect
Attribute: Wind
Level: 4
ATK: 1200
DEF: 1000
Rarity: Common

No matter the opponent, one poisonous sting from this giant bee and it's history. If they ever swarm you, then duck underwater!

MRD-007 Larvae Moth

Card Type: Effect Monster
Monster Type: Insect
Attribute: Earth
Level: 2
ATK: 500
DEF: 400
Rarity: Common

"Larvae Moth" is the first stage of evolution of "Petit Moth." In order to evolve, it rests in a tree's shadows and gathers its strength. When offering "Cocoon of Evolution," you must have "Larvae Moth" in your hand.

MRD-008 Harpie Lady

Card Type: Normal Monster
Monster Type: Winged Beast
Attribute: Wind
Level: 4
ATK: 1300
DEF: 1400
Rarity: Common

This Winged Beast has average ATK and DEF, but it is indispensable in Summoning "Harpie Lady Sisters!"

MRD-009 Harpie Lady Sisters

Card Type: Effect Monster
Monster Type: Winged Beast
Attribute: Wind
Level: 6
ATK: 1950
DEF: 2100
Rarity: Super Rare

Special Summon "Harpie Lady Sisters" using "Elegant Egotist." It has both high ATK and DEF, so it is a force to be reckoned with!

MRD-010 Kojikocy

Card Type: Normal Monster

Monster Type: Warrior

Attribute: Earth

Level: 4

ATK: 1500

DEF: 1200

Rarity: Common

This Warrior has extremely powerful destructive powers! It will definitely be a core force in Warrior-Type Decks.

MRD-011 Cocoon of Evolution

Card Type: Effect Monster

Monster Type: Insect

Attribute: Earth

Level: 3

ATK: 0

DEF: 2000

Rarity: Common

"Cocoon of Evolution" is an Effect Monster Card that you can equip to "Petit Moth." You can Normal Summon this Monster although you cannot equip it to "Petit Moth" once it is Normal Summoned and vice versa.

MRD-012 Crawling Dragon

Card Type: Normal Monster

Monster Type: Dragon

Attribute: Earth

Level: 5

ATK: 1600

DEF: 1400

Rarity: Common

This Dragon has been around from the dawn of time, so maybe you should leave this living artifact alone instead of destroying it.

MRD-013 Armored Zombie

Card Type: Normal Monster

Monster Type: Zombie

Attribute: Dark

Level: 3

ATK: 1500

DEF: 0

Rarity: Common

Strong grudges prevented this armored warrior from moving on to the next world. With no reasoning left, all it can do is swing its sword.

MRD-014 Mask of Darkness

Card Type: Effect Monster

Monster Type: Fiend

Attribute: Dark

Level: 2

ATK: 900

DEF: 400

Rarity: Rare

While "Mask of Darkness" can resurrect Trap Cards from the Graveyard, if there are no Trap Cards in the Graveyard, then you cannot recover anything.

MRD-015 Doma The Angel of Silence

Card Type: Normal Monster

Monster Type: Fairy

Attribute: Dark

Level: 5

ATK: 1600

DEF: 1400

Rarity: Common

A Fairy with DARK, this creature is full of mystery. You must offer one Monster as a Tribute to Summon this Monster.

MRD-016 White Magical Hat

Card Type: Effect Monster

Monster Type: Spellcaster

Attribute: Light

Level: 3

ATK: 1000

DEF: 700

Rarity: Rare

This strange Spellcaster appears when the moon is in the sky and only steals from crooks. While its ATK is mediocre, its ability to force your opponent to discard cards from his or her hand is immeasurable. This is especially useful when your opponent is trying to set up a combo.

MRD-017 Big Eye

Card Type: Effect Monster

Monster Type: Fiend

Attribute: Dark

Level: 4

ATK: 1200

DEF: 1000

Rarity: Common

Using all its eyes on its body, this Fiend can see into the future. It can anticipate its opponent's next move to dodge attacks. If your Deck is a Combo Deck, this card makes things interesting. You can draw the exact cards you need earlier, allowing you to form strategies easier. However, "Big Eye" does not go well with cards that require you to shuffle the Deck.

MRD-018 B. Skull Dragon

Card Type: Fusion Monster

Monster Type: Dragon

Attribute: Dark

Level: 9

ATK: 3200

DEF: 2500

Rarity: Ultra Rare

Create one of the fiercest Monsters in action by fusing "Summoned Skull" and "Red-Eyes B. Dragon" with "Polymerization." This must-have card has capabilities for powerful combos.

MRD-019 Masked Sorcerer

Card Type: Effect Monster
Monster Type: Spellcaster
Attribute: Dark
Level: 4
ATK: 900
DEF: 1400
Rarity: Rare

A sorcerer adorned with relics from an ancient civilization, he gained the ability to see the future through a steel mask. No one has ever seen his face. With this card, you can prevent losing cards from your hand. "Masked Sorcerer" works well with "Muka Muka," so they should be put into the same Deck. However, it may be hard to get an attack through.

MRD-020 Roaring Ocean Snake

Card Type: Fusion Monster
Monster Type: Aqua
Attribute: Water
Level: 6
ATK: 2100
DEF: 1800
Rarity: Common

Create "Roaring Ocean Snake" by fusing "Mystic Lamp" and "Hyosube" using "Polymerization." Since its Fusion-Material Monsters are weak, "Roaring Ocean Snake" is not the easiest Monster to Summon, but its ATK is certainly attractive.

MRD-021 Water Omotics

Card Type: Normal Monster
Monster Type: Aqua
Attribute: Water
Level: 4
ATK: 1400
DEF: 1200
Rarity: Common

This water fairy loves dragons. Don't try to sneak up on her unless you're ready to receive punishment.

MRD-022 Ground Attacker Bugroth

Card Type: Normal Monster
Monster Type: Machine
Attribute: Earth
Level: 4
ATK: 1500
DEF: 1000
Rarity: Common

Although "Ground Attacker Bugroth" is a high-performance Machine, it's easy to Summon because it's a Level 4 Monster! Hit-and-run tactics are its strength!

MRD-023 Petit Moth

Card Type: Normal Monster
Monster Type: Insect
Attribute: Earth
Level: 1
ATK: 300
DEF: 200
Rarity: Common

No one knows what this Insect will evolve into. "Petit Moth" is a challenging card to use.

MRD-024 Elegant Egotist

Card Type: Spell
Monster Type: —
Attribute: Spell
Level: —
ATK: —
DEF: —
Rarity: Rare

After Special Summoning "Harpie Lady Sisters," don't forget to shuffle your Deck.

MRD-025 Sanga of the Thunder

Card Type: Effect Monster
Monster Type: Thunder
Attribute: Light
Level: 7
ATK: 2600
DEF: 2200
Rarity: Super Rare

"Sanga of the Thunder" is the strongest of the three deities. Since it has an electrical current constantly running on the surface of its body, its special powers block damage from opponents that touch it. If your opponent Summons a powerful Monster that you are not prepared for, "Sanga of the Thunder's" effect can buy you time to draw a useful card from your Deck.

MRD-026 Kazejin

Card Type: Effect Monster
Monster Type: Spellcaster
Attribute: Wind
Level: 7
ATK: 2400
DEF: 2200
Rarity: Super Rare

A rare Spellcaster with WIND, "Kazejin" uses its own breath to create a wall of air to stop its opponent's attacks. Though it is not as powerful as "Sanga of the Thunder" and "Suijin," "Kazejin" has the ability to make the ATK of an opponent's Monster 0. However, you have to ask yourself if it's worth it to offer two Monsters as a Tribute to Summon "Kazejin." If you do Summon this Monster, then definitely attack!

MRD-027 Suijin

Card Type: Effect Monster
Monster Type: Aqua
Attribute: Water
Level: 7
ATK: 2500
DEF: 2400
Rarity: Super Rare

This magical deity gathers water spirits. WATER Monsters usually lack ATK, but "Suijin" boasts incredible ATK. It negates your opponent's attacks with a wall of water. Even if your opponent attacks with "Summoned Skull," "Suijin" will survive while "Summoned Skull" will not if you use "Suijin's" effect. The only drawback is that you need to offer two Monsters as a Tribute to Summon "Suijin."

MRD-028 Mystic Lamp

Card Type:
Effect Monster

Monster Type:
Spellcaster

Attribute:
Dark

Level: 1

ATK: 400

DEF: 300

Rarity: Common

When you rub this legendary lamp, a genie appears and makes your wishes come true. "Mystic Lamp" also serves as Fusion-Material for "Roaring Ocean Snake." You can fuse this card with "Hyosube," attack your opponent directly, or use it for defense. "Mystic Lamp" is versatile, so it can be quite useful.

MRD-029 Steel Scorpion

Card Type:
Effect Monster

Monster Type:
Machine

Attribute:
Earth

Level: 1

ATK: 250

DEF: 300

Rarity: Common

This Monster is very weak but even "Summoned Skull" cannot avoid this effect when it attacks this Monster.

MRD-030 Ocubeam

Card Type:
Normal Monster

Monster Type:
Fairy

Attribute:
Light

Level: 5

ATK: 1550

DEF: 1650

Rarity: Common

Even though "Ocubeam" has high ATK and DEF, you must offer a Monster as a Tribute to Summon this high-level Monster. However, you'll be glad to have "Ocubeam" on your Field if you can Summon it!

MRD-031 Leghul

Card Type:
Effect Monster

Monster Type:
Insect

Attribute:
Earth

Level: 1

ATK: 300

DEF: 350

Rarity: Common

This pesky Insect pokes enemies with its sharp spikes. Sometimes, it goes unnoticed by large enemies and simply ends up being stamped on. You probably won't use this card unless you power it up with plenty of Spell and Trap Cards. This card is usually used in Decks that destroy your opponent's hand or Decks that contain "Cannon Soldier."

MRD-032 Ooguchi

Card Type:
Effect Monster

Monster Type:
Aqua

Attribute:
Water

Level: 1

ATK: 300

DEF: 250

Rarity: Common

This Monster suddenly bites you with its huge mouth from underwater. However, since it's usually an herbivore, its fangs have deteriorated. After using "Swords of Revealing Light," "Ooguchi" can be quite a force with "Cannon Soldier." If you attack and then offer it as a Tribute to "Cannon Soldier," you can cause significant damage to your opponent's Life Points.

MRD-033 Leogun

Card Type:
Normal Monster

Monster Type:
Beast

Attribute:
Earth

Level: 5

ATK: 1750

DEF: 1550

Rarity: Common

A giant lion with a trademark golden mane, "Leogun" is extremely ferocious and will mercilessly fight even a weakened opponent.

MRD-034 Blast Juggler

Card Type:
Effect Monster

Monster Type:
Machine

Attribute:
Fire

Level: 3

ATK: 800

DEF: 900

Rarity: Common

This walking explosive destroys all enemies within its range. You can destroy annoying Effect Monsters in one full sweep, but if left in Attack Position, you can expect your opponent to retaliate. Include this card in your Deck if you have very little removal cards.

MRD-035 Jinzo #7

Card Type:
Effect Monster

Monster Type:
Machine

Attribute:
Dark

Level: 2

ATK: 500

DEF: 400

Rarity: Common

Since this android, created by science, lacks a heart, it feels no pain. It's a horrific creature that continues its carnage until it's destroyed. "Jinzo #7" has one of the highest ATK for a direct damage Monster. After powering it up with "Sword of Deep-Seated," force your opponent to lose cards in his or her hand by using "Robbin' Goblin."

MRD-036 Magician of Faith

Card Type:
Effect Monster

Monster Type:
Spellcaster

Attribute:
Light

Level: 1

ATK: 300

DEF: 400

Rarity: Rare

Similar to "Mask of Darkness," "Magician of Faith" can resurrect Spell Cards. Use "Magician of Faith" after using a powerful Spell Card.

Card Catalog

MRD-037 Ancient Elf

Card Type:
Normal Monster

Monster Type:
Spellcaster

Attribute:
Light

Level: 4

ATK: 1450

DEF: 1200

Rarity: Common

Rumors say this elf has lived for millenniums.

MRD-038 Deepsea Shark

Card Type:
Fusion Monster

Monster Type:
Fish

Attribute:
Water

Level: 5

ATK: 1900

DEF: 1600

Rarity: Common

Create this gigantic shark that lives at the bottom of the ocean by fusing "Bottom Dweller" and "Tongyo" with "Polymerization."

MRD-039 Bottom Dweller

Card Type:
Normal Monster

Monster Type:
Fish

Attribute:
Water

Level: 5

ATK: 1650

DEF: 1700

Rarity: Common

It's quite a challenge to Summon this long-lived Fish, but it is certainly worth it when you see it in battle!

MRD-040 Destroyer Golem

Card Type:
Normal Monster

Monster Type:
Rock

Attribute:
Earth

Level: 4

ATK: 1500

DEF: 1000

Rarity: Common

You can count on "Destroyer Golem's" high ATK in combat, but beware—its DEF is surprisingly low!

MRD-041 Kaminari Attack

Card Type:
Fusion Monster

Monster Type:
Thunder

Attribute:
Wind

Level: 5

ATK: 1900

DEF: 1400

Rarity: Common

The Fusion-Material Monsters for this Thunder-Type Fusion Monster are weak, so have the Monster Cards in your hand when you use "Polymerization" to Summon "Kaminari Attack."

MRD-042 Rainbow Flower

Card Type:
Effect Monster

Monster Type:
Plant

Attribute:
Earth

Level: 2

ATK: 400

DEF: 500

Rarity: Common

Looks can be deceiving! This eerie flower launches an attack just when its opponent's fears are put to rest by its cute looks. While it can attack the opponent's Life Points directly, it can be destroyed easily next turn because it has low ATK. If you are going to use this card, attack after using "Swords of Revealing Light" first.

MRD-043 Morinphen

Card Type:
Normal Monster

Monster Type:
Fiend

Attribute:
Dark

Level: 5

ATK: 1550

DEF: 1300

Rarity: Common

This strange Fiend, born in the depths of shadows, has long arms and razor-sharp talons.

MRD-044 Mega Thunderball

Card Type:
Normal Monster

Monster Type:
Thunder

Attribute:
Wind

Level: 2

ATK: 750

DEF: 600

Rarity: Common

Since "Mega Thunderball" accumulates so much electricity when it's not moving, it constantly rolls around to expend the extra electricity.

MRD-045 Tongyo

Card Type:
Normal Monster

Monster Type:
Fish

Attribute:
Water

Level: 4

ATK: 1350

DEF: 800

Rarity: Common

"Tongyo" sneaks up from behind and wraps its long tongue around its enemy! If you get caught, it's hard to break free.

MRD-046 Empress Judge

Card Type: Fusion Monster
Monster Type: Warrior
Attribute: Earth
Level: 6
ATK: 2100
DEF: 1700
Rarity: Common

Created by fusing "Queens' Double" and "Hibikime" by "Polymerization," she possesses high-ranking attack powers among all female Warriors. Rumor says she was once an empress who ruled an ancient Eastern land.

MRD-047 Pale Beast

Card Type: Normal Monster
Monster Type: Beast
Attribute: Earth
Level: 4
ATK: 1500
DEF: 1200
Rarity: Common

Living deep in the shadows of a forest, the pair of eyes on "Pale Beast's" chin help it find prey.

MRD-048 Electric Lizard

Card Type: Effect Monster
Monster Type: Thunder
Attribute: Earth
Level: 3
ATK: 850
DEF: 800
Rarity: Common

"Electric Lizard's" effect is useful, but afterwards, it's only useful for being offered as a Tribute for a stronger Monster if it is not destroyed by the attack from an opponent's Monster.

MRD-049 Hunter Spider

Card Type: Normal Monster
Monster Type: Insect
Attribute: Earth
Level: 5
ATK: 1600
DEF: 1400
Rarity: Common

This spider is not only strong but also quite intelligent! You'll be finished if you find yourself wrapped up in its web.

MRD-050 Ancient Lizard Warrior

Card Type: Normal Monster
Monster Type: Reptile
Attribute: Earth
Level: 4
ATK: 1400
DEF: 1100
Rarity: Common

These warriors are true to their ancient ways, refining their skills with their one-of-a-kind training method.

MRD-051 Queen's Double

Card Type: Effect Monster
Monster Type: Warrior
Attribute: Earth
Level: 1
ATK: 350
DEF: 300
Rarity: Common

"Queen's Double" is a soldier who protects the queen of a prosperous Eastern land. Expertly wielding a knife, she pretends to be the queen to protect her from would-be kidnappers. "Queen's Double" can not only attack your opponent directly, but it is also a Fusion-Material Monster for "Empress Judge." This card works well with "Robbin' Goblin," so use them in the same Deck.

MRD-052 Trent

Card Type: Normal Monster
Monster Type: Plant
Attribute: Earth
Level: 5
ATK: 1500
DEF: 1800
Rarity: Common

"Trent's" DEF is pretty good, but since it requires a Tribute to Summon, using this card is a tough call.

MRD-053 Disk Magician

Card Type: Normal Monster
Monster Type: Machine
Attribute: Dark
Level: 4
ATK: 1350
DEF: 1000
Rarity: Common

If you approach the disk, the magician spontaneously appears and attacks. You can often find it guarding ancient ruins and fighting off invaders.

MRD-054 Hyosube

Card Type: Normal Monster
Monster Type: Aqua
Attribute: Water
Level: 4
ATK: 1500
DEF: 900
Rarity: Common

When viewed alone, neither its ATK or DEF are impressive. However, it is useful as Fusion-Material for Summoning "Roaring Ocean Snake."

MRD-055 Hibikime

Card Type: Normal Monster
Monster Type: Warrior
Attribute: Earth
Level: 4
ATK: 1450
DEF: 1000
Rarity: Common

This female Warrior prides herself in her ability to emit unpleasant sounds that confuse her opponents. Though she's not powerful on her own, she is Fusion-Material for "Empress Judge."

MRD-056 Fake Trap

Card Type: Trap
Monster Type: —
Attribute: Trap
Level: —
ATK: —
DEF: —
Rarity: Rare

Use this Trap Card to fool your opponent. It's fun to watch your opponent squirm while he or she thinks this card's a Trap Card. However, this card is useless by itself. Fake Trap can protect all your other Trap Cards, making this card indispensable.

MRD-057 Tribute to The Doomed

Card Type: Spell
Monster Type: —
Attribute: Spell
Level: —
ATK: —
DEF: —
Rarity: Super Rare

In ancient Egypt, it was customary to offer tributes upon the Pharaoh's demise, a custom that exists to the present. "Tribute to the Doomed" forces you to discard one card from your hand, but that's not a high price to pay considering that you can destroy your opponent's most powerful Monster. It can also destroy Flip Effect Monster Cards without activating their effects.

MRD-058 Soul Release

Card Type: Spell
Monster Type: —
Attribute: Spell
Level: —
ATK: —
DEF: —
Rarity: Common

Free this wandering soul so that it can move on to the spirit world. "Soul Release" prevents powerful Monster, Spell, and Trap Cards from being reused by removing cards in the Graveyard from play. Use it as countermeasure against "Monster Reborn"-"Magician of Faith" combos.

MRD-059 The Cheerful Coffin

Card Type: Spell
Monster Type: —
Attribute: Spell
Level: —
ATK: —
DEF: —
Rarity: Common

A mortician never goes out of business in any day or age. They appear out of nowhere and bury our dead with a smile. You can discard hard-to-Summon Monsters in the Graveyard, and then revive them with "Monster Reborn." However, this magic is less effective against "Tribute to the Doomed."

MRD-060 Change of Heart

Card Type: Spell
Monster Type: —
Attribute: Spell
Level: —
ATK: —
DEF: —
Rarity: Ultra Rare

The heart is a transient thing, and this is true for Monsters' hearts as well - so much that Monsters at times forget who their masters are. The Monster you worked so hard to Summon suddenly defects to your opponent. This effect lasts only the turn "Change of Heart" is activated, so the Monster is often offered as a Tribute.

MRD-061 Baby Dragon

Card Type: Normal Monster
Monster Type: Dragon
Attribute: Wind
Level: 3
ATK: 1200
DEF: 700
Rarity: Common

Though "Baby Dragon" is still a baby, it has huge potential for power. Fuse "Baby Dragon" with "Time Wizard" to Summon "Thousand Dragon!"

MRD-062 Blackland Fire Dragon

Card Type: Normal Monster
Monster Type: Dragon
Attribute: Dark
Level: 4
ATK: 1500
DEF: 800
Rarity: Common

This Dragon lives in the depths of shadows, so it has poor eyesight. However, it more than makes up for it with its keen sense of smell to locate its prey.

MRD-063 Swamp Battleguard

Card Type: Effect Monster
Monster Type: Warrior
Attribute: Earth
Level: 5
ATK: 1800
DEF: 1500
Rarity: Common

This card shows its true colors when it's on the Field with "Lava Battleguard," so placing this Monster on the Field alone is pointless. "Swamp Battleguard" is the offensive arm of the Battleguard brothers. If it is on the Field with "Lava Battleguard," its ATK increases by 500 points to 2300. The only catch is that this Monster is a Tribute Summon.

MRD-064 Battle Steer

Card Type:
Normal Monster

Monster Type:
Beast-Warrior

Attribute:
Earth

Level: 5

ATK: 1800

DEF: 1300

Rarity: Common

A Monster in the form of a steer, "Battle Steer" charges its enemies with its horns. It is constantly excited by the red cape it has wrapped around itself.

MRD-065 Time Wizard

Card Type:
Effect Monster

Monster Type:
Spellcaster

Attribute:
Light

Level: 2

ATK: 500

DEF: 400

Rarity: Ultra Rare

This Spellcaster has the ability to control time. Fuse "Time Wizard" with "Baby Dragon" to Summon "Thousand Dragon."

MRD-066 Saggi the Dark Clown

Card Type:
Normal Monster

Monster Type:
Spellcaster

Attribute:
Dark

Level: 3

ATK: 600

DEF: 1500

Rarity: Common

This elusive clown appears out of nowhere, so if you hear an eerie laugh, watch out because chances are that "Saggi the Dark Clown" is nearby!

MRD-067 Dragon Piper

Card Type:
Effect Monster

Monster Type:
Pyro

Attribute:
Fire

Level: 3

ATK: 200

DEF: 1800

Rarity: Common

If you have a Dragon-Type Deck, place "Dragon Piper" in your Side Deck in case your opponent has "Dragon Capture Jar." However, the Spell Card "Remove Trap" may be more versatile....

MRD-068 Illusionist Faceless Mage

Card Type:
Normal Monster

Monster Type:
Spellcaster

Attribute:
Dark

Level: 5

ATK: 1200

DEF: 2200

Rarity: Common

You won't regret offering a Monster as a Tribute to Summon this Spellcaster with high DEF. As long as you have its defenses, you're in good health.

MRD-069 Sangan

Card Type:
Effect Monster

Monster Type:
Fiend

Attribute:
Dark

Level: 3

ATK: 1000

DEF: 600

Rarity: Rare

Similar to "Witch of the Black Forest," you cannot draw a Monster with high ATK, but there are many Effect Monsters that may be useful.

MRD-070 Great Moth

Card Type:
Effect Monster

Monster Type:
Insect

Attribute:
Earth

Level: 8

ATK: 2600

DEF: 2500

Rarity: Rare

There are many Monster removal cards, so you will find it difficult to protect "Petit Moth" for four turns. Therefore, construct a Deck designed to protect "Petit Moth" in order to Special Summon "Great Moth."

MRD-071 Kuriboh

Card Type:
Effect Monster

Monster Type:
Fiend

Attribute:
Dark

Level: 1

ATK: 300

DEF: 200

Rarity: Super Rare

This card acts as a shield for your Life Points. When you're in a difficult situation, add this card to your hand using "Witch of the Black Forest" or "Sangan."

MRD-072 Jellyfish

Card Type:
Normal Monster

Monster Type:
Aqua

Attribute:
Water

Level: 4

ATK: 1200

DEF: 1500

Rarity: Common

This Monster was used by Mako Tsunami. This semi-transparent creature drifts in the sea.

Card Catalog

MRD-073 Castle of Dark Illusions

Card Type: Effect Monster
Monster Type: Fiend
Attribute: Dark
Level: 4
ATK: 920
DEF: 1930
Rarity: Common

If your Deck contains many Zombie-Type Monsters, then your Monsters will power up. If you buy time with "Swords of Revealing Light," your advantage further increases.

MRD-074 King of Yamimakai

Card Type: Normal Monster
Monster Type: Fiend
Attribute: Dark
Level: 5
ATK: 2000
DEF: 1530
Rarity: Common

One of the Fiend kings of the underworld, he has no eyes because he prefers the pitch-black Yami Field.

MRD-075 Catapult Turtle

Card Type: Effect Monster
Monster Type: Aqua
Attribute: Water
Level: 5
ATK: 1000
DEF: 2000
Rarity: Super Rare

"Catapult Turtle" is a beefed-up version of "Cannon Soldier." It requires a Tribute to Summon, but you can Special Summon it with "Last Will." If you can lock down a combo with "Ultimate Offering," the battle will be yours for the taking.

MRD-076 Mystic Horseman

Card Type: Normal Monster
Monster Type: Beast
Attribute: Earth
Level: 4
ATK: 1300
DEF: 1550
Rarity: Common

This legendary creature is half-man, half-horse. It can run very fast, making it ideal for swift attacks.

MRD-077 Rabid Horseman

Card Type: Fusion Monster
Monster Type: Beast-Warrior
Attribute: Earth
Level: 6
ATK: 2000
DEF: 1700
Rarity: Common

Created by fusing "Battle Ox" and "Mystic Horseman" using "Polymerization," this relentless Beast-Warrior possesses horrendous destructive capabilities as well as speed and grace.

MRD-078 Crass Clown

Card Type: Effect Monster
Monster Type: Fiend
Attribute: Dark
Level: 4
ATK: 1350
DEF: 1400
Rarity: Common

When first Summoned face-down and then switched to Attack Position, then it is similar to "Hane-Hane." It's a question of whether you can use this effect again, but it has much higher ATK than "Hane-Hane," so "Crass Clown" may be better.

MRD-079 Pumpking the King of Ghosts

Card Type: Effect Monster
Monster Type: Zombie
Attribute: Dark
Level: 6
ATK: 1800
DEF: 2000
Rarity: Common

When combined with "Castle of Dark Illusions'" effect, "Pumpking the King of Ghosts'" ATK and DEF increase by 100 every turn! If you can make it last five turns, it will have 2300 ATK and 2500 DEF! But remember that even if you have two "Castle of Dark Illusions," you cannot double this card's effect.

MRD-080 Dream Clown

Card Type: Effect Monster
Monster Type: Warrior
Attribute: Earth
Level: 3
ATK: 1200
DEF: 900
Rarity: Common

Since its ATK is low, "Dream Clown" can be easily destroyed before it can activate its effect. However, the effect is very useful. Try using this in a Deck with "Swords of Revealing Light."

MRD-081 Tainted Wisdom

Card Type: Effect Monster
Monster Type: Fiend
Attribute: Dark
Level: 3
ATK: 1250
DEF: 800
Rarity: Common

In order to use this card's effect, it must first be in Attack Position. However, since it has relatively low ATK, it can be easily destroyed...and its effect isn't that great.

MRD-082 Ancient Brain

Card Type: Normal Monster
Monster Type: Fiend
Attribute: Dark
Level: 3
ATK: 1000
DEF: 700
Rarity: Common

This fallen angel was exiled from the heavens due to his research into forbidden evil wisdom. Its brain is large due to the massive amount of information it has acquired.

MRD-083 Guardian of the Labyrinth

Card Type: Normal Monster
Monster Type: Warrior
Attribute: Earth
Level: 4
ATK: 1000
DEF: 1200
Rarity: Common

This Monster guards the entrance to the underworld with "Flame Cerebrus." His shield has a mouth that can also attack.

MRD-084 Prevent Rat

Card Type: Normal Monster
Monster Type: Beast
Attribute: Earth
Level: 4
ATK: 500
DEF: 2000
Rarity: Common

This Monster has 2000 DEF! Use this card to protect your Life Points.

MRD-085 The Little Swordsman of Aile

Card Type: Effect Monster
Monster Type: Warrior
Attribute: Water
Level: 3
ATK: 800
DEF: 1300
Rarity: Common

If you have Flip Effect Monsters or other Monsters that are useless in battle, then use them to power up "The Little Swordsman of Aile" and attack. If you offer two Monsters as a Tribute, there will be plenty of damage!

MRD-086 Princess of Tsurugi

Card Type: Effect Monster
Monster Type: Warrior
Attribute: Wind
Level: 3
ATK: 900
DEF: 700
Rarity: Rare

Princess of Tsurugi is very effective against opponents who use many Spell and Trap Cards. If used correctly, you can eliminate almost half your opponent's Life Points.

MRD-087 Protector of the Throne

Card Type: Normal Monster
Monster Type: Warrior
Attribute: Earth
Level: 4
ATK: 800
DEF: 1500
Rarity: Common

This queen protects the royal throne while the king is away. The floating crystal possesses various powers that protect the queen from enemies.

MRD-088 Tremendous Fire

Card Type: Spell
Monster Type: —
Attribute: Spell
Level: —
ATK: —
DEF: —
Rarity: Common

Even if you receive 500 damage, dealing 1000 damage is a good deal. If your opponent has less than 1000 Life Points, this can be the finishing blow!

MRD-089 Jirai Gumo

Card Type: Effect Monster
Monster Type: Insect
Attribute: Earth
Level: 4
ATK: 2200
DEF: 100
Rarity: Common

Its ATK are incredible and you don't have to offer another Monster as a Tribute! However, the risk is huge! It may be good to attack if you're close to defeat, but until then, it may be best to leave it for protecting your Life Points.

MRD-090 Shadow Ghoul

Card Type: Effect Monster
Monster Type: Zombie
Attribute: Dark
Level: 5
ATK: 1600
DEF: 1300
Rarity: Rare

Summon "Shadow Ghoul" when you have a lot of Monsters in your Graveyard. This card works well in Decks that contain "Cannon Soldier" and "Catapult Turtle" because they discard Monsters into the Graveyard.

Card Catalog

MRD-091 Labyrinth Tank

Card Type: Fusion Monster
Monster Type: Machine
Attribute: Dark
Level: 7
ATK: 2400
DEF: 2400
Rarity: Common

Create "Labyrinth Tank" by fusing "Giga-Tech Wolf" and "Cannon Soldier" using "Polymerization." This tank destroys anyone who enters the labyrinth. However, even the tank itself gets lost in the maze....

MRD-092 Ryu-Kishin Powered

Card Type: Normal Monster
Monster Type: Fiend
Attribute: Dark
Level: 4
ATK: 1600
DEF: 1200
Rarity: Common

Kaiba uses this beefed-up version of "Ryu-Kishin." Its armorlike body and huge sharp claws power up its abilities.

MRD-093 Bickuribox

Card Type: Fusion Monster
Monster Type: Fiend
Attribute: Dark
Level: 7
ATK: 2300
DEF: 2000
Rarity: Common

Create "Bickuribox" by fusing "Crass Clown" and "Dream Clown" with "Polymerization." This Fiend jumps out and attacks anyone that gets near its toy box.

MRD-094 Giltia the D. Knight

Card Type: Fusion Monster
Monster Type: Warrior
Attribute: Light
Level: 5
ATK: 1850
DEF: 1500
Rarity: Common

Fuse "Guardian of the Labyrinth" and "Protector of the Throne" by "Polymerization" to create this Warrior who is also adept at magic. He infuses his magic into his weapon to increase its power.

MRD-095 Launcher Spider

Card Type: Normal Monster
Monster Type: Machine
Attribute: Fire
Level: 7
ATK: 2200
DEF: 2500
Rarity: Common

This Machine-Type Monster recklessly launches super-powerful rockets. Though you need to offer two Monsters as a Tribute to Summon "Launcher Spider," its ATK and DEF are certainly attractive.

MRD-096 Giga-Tech Wolf

Card Type: Normal Monster
Monster Type: Machine
Attribute: Fire
Level: 4
ATK: 1200
DEF: 1400
Rarity: Common

This cyborg wolf is made entirely of steel and can unleash various attacks using its wings and each of its arrowhead tails.

MRD-097 Thunder Dragon

Card Type: Effect Monster
Monster Type: Thunder
Attribute: Light
Level: 5
ATK: 1600
DEF: 1500
Rarity: Common

If you have this card and "Polymerization" in your hand, you can immediately Summon the powerful Fusion Monster "Twin-Headed Thunder Dragon!" You can only use this effect once, but it still powerful!

MRD-098 7 Colored Fish

Card Type: Normal Monster
Monster Type: Fish
Attribute: Water
Level: 4
ATK: 1800
DEF: 800
Rarity: Common

"7 Colored Fish" is extremely powerful for a Monster that does not have to be a Tribute Summon. Everyone should get this card!

MRD-099 The Immortal of Thunder

Card Type: Effect Monster
Monster Type: Thunder
Attribute: Light
Level: 4
ATK: 1500
DEF: 1300
Rarity: Common

This card acts like a bank for Life Points. When you want to use a Spell, Trap, or Effect Monster Card that requires you to spend Life Points, then "The Immortal of Thunder" gives you a temporary life boost. However, if it is attacked and destroyed, you end up losing 2000 points.

TRADING CARD GAME

MRD-100 Punished Eagle

Card Type:
Fusion Monster

Monster Type:
Winged Beast

Attribute:
Wind

Level: 6

ATK: 2100

DEF: 1800

Rarity: Common

Summon "Punished Eagle" by fusing "Blue-Winged Crown" and "Niwatori" using "Polymerization." This eagle was sent from above to judge humans. It creates an enormous tornado with a single flap of its wings.

MRD-101 Insect Soldiers of the Sky

Card Type:
Effect Monster

Monster Type:
Insect

Attribute:
Wind

Level: 3

ATK: 1000

DEF: 800

Rarity: Common

Definitely give this card a shot if your opponent is using WIND Monsters. However, its original ATK is low, so beware. Once it powers up, then it is a force to be reckoned with.

MRD-102 Hoshiningen

Card Type:
Effect Monster

Monster Type:
Fairy

Attribute:
Light

Level: 2

ATK: 500

DEF: 700

Rarity: Rare

Most LIGHT Monsters have low ATK, so this card's effect may not be very effective.

MRD-103 Musician King

Card Type:
Fusion Monster

Monster Type:
Spellcaster

Attribute:
Light

Level: 5

ATK: 1750

DEF: 1500

Rarity: Common

Create "Musician King" by fusing "Witch of the Black Forest" and "Lady of Faith" using "Polymerization." It attacks its enemies with loud sound waves. Its trademarks are its bandanna and guitar.

MRD-104 Yado Karu

Card Type:
Effect Monster

Monster Type:
Aqua

Attribute:
Water

Level: 4

ATK: 900

DEF: 1700

Rarity: Common

Put cards that cannot help you currently at the bottom of your Deck. But be careful not to put a card back in your Deck that you may need real soon....

MRD-105 Cyber Saurus

Card Type:
Fusion Monster

Monster Type:
Machine

Attribute:
Earth

Level: 5

ATK: 1800

DEF: 1400

Rarity: Common

Created by fusing "Blast Juggler" and "Two-Headed King Rex" by "Polymerization," this artificially created dinosaur's body is 90 percent machine.

MRD-106 Cannon Soldier

Card Type:
Effect Monster

Monster Type:
Machine

Attribute:
Dark

Level: 4

ATK: 1400

DEF: 1300

Rarity: Rare

"Cannon Soldier" can offer itself as a Tribute. This card works effectively with Monsters that are useless in battle, Effect Monsters whose effects have already been triggered, or cards like "Sangan" and "Witch of the Black Forest" that allow you to add more Monsters from your Deck when they are sent to the Graveyard.

MRD-107 Muka Muka

Card Type:
Effect Monster

Monster Type:
Rock

Attribute:
Earth

Level: 2

ATK: 600

DEF: 300

Rarity: Rare

If you Summon "Muka Muka" on your first turn, you just Summoned a Monster with 2100 ATK! Afterwards, try to keep as many cards in your hand. If you need to use a card, then attack first.

MRD-108 The Bistro Butcher

Card Type:
Effect Monster

Monster Type:
Fiend

Attribute:
Dark

Level: 4

ATK: 1800

DEF: 1000

Rarity: Common

You may think it's a drawback to allow your opponent to draw two cards, but if you combine "The Bistro Butcher" with other cards that remove cards from your opponent's hand and Deck, you will make your opponent runs out of cards faster!

Card Catalog

MRD-109 Star Boy

Card Type: **Effect Monster**

Monster Type: **Aqua**

Attribute: **Water**

Level: **2**

ATK: **550**

DEF: **500**

Rarity: **Rare**

If you play with the rarely-used WATER Monster, then "Star Boy's" effect won't affect your opponent's cards and will only power your Monsters up. Your main force will be "7 Colored Fish" with 1800 ATK.

MRD-110 Milus Radiant

Card Type: **Effect Monster**

Monster Type: **Beast**

Attribute: **Earth**

Level: **1**

ATK: **300**

DEF: **250**

Rarity: **Rare**

When you use this card, all EARTH Monsters gain 500 ATK while all WIND Monsters lose 400 ATK. This effect affects "Milus Radiant" itself.

MRD-111 Flame Cerebrus

Card Type: **Normal Monster**

Monster Type: **Pyro**

Attribute: **Fire**

Level: **6**

ATK: **2100**

DEF: **1800**

Rarity: **Common**

Ranking quite high among Level 6 Monsters, it destroys its enemies with its three pairs of jaws and burning flame. No Level 4 Monster can stand up against it.

MRD-112 Niwatori

Card Type: **Normal Monster**

Monster Type: **Winged Beast**

Attribute: **Earth**

Level: **3**

ATK: **900**

DEF: **800**

Rarity: **Common**

This bird swallows enemies whole and coverts them into energy. It's stomach is so big it can swallow anything!

MRD-113 Dark Elf

Card Type: **Effect Monster**

Monster Type: **Spellcaster**

Attribute: **Dark**

Level: **4**

ATK: **2000**

DEF: **800**

Rarity: **Rare**

Finally, here's a Level 4 Monster that has 2000 ATK. However, it functions as a wall in Attack Position. Paying 1000 Life Points to attack is usually only useful when your opponent has no Monsters on the Field.

MRD-114 Mushroom Man #2

Card Type: **Effect Monster**

Monster Type: **Warrior**

Attribute: **Earth**

Level: **3**

ATK: **1250**

DEF: **800**

Rarity: **Common**

Having "Mushroom Man #2" on the Field and tossing it back between you and your opponent can be fun. This card may be just for fun, but it can be cool to find a good use for this card.

MRD-115 Lava Battleguard

Card Type: **Effect Monster**

Monster Type: **Warrior**

Attribute: **Earth**

Level: **5**

ATK: **1550**

DEF: **1800**

Rarity: **Common**

"Lava Battleguard" exerts its true powers when it's on the Field with "Swamp Battleguard." "Lava Battleguard's" DEF is higher than its ATK, so it is better suited for defense. However, if "Swamp Battleguard" is also on the Field, then its ATK increases by 500, making "Lava Battleguard" suited to attack.

MRD-116 Witch of the Black Forest

Card Type: **Effect Monster**

Monster Type: **Spellcaster**

Attribute: **Dark**

Level: **4**

ATK: **1100**

DEF: **1200**

Rarity: **Rare**

You can draw most Effect Monster Cards from your Deck while thinning out your Deck at the same time. Also, less than 1500 DEF means that you can add "Summoned Skull" from your Deck!

MRD-117 Little Chimera

Card Type: **Effect Monster**

Monster Type: **Beast**

Attribute: **Fire**

Level: **2**

ATK: **600**

DEF: **550**

Rarity: **Rare**

Use "Little Chimera" in your Deck if you can easily Summon FIRE Monsters or if your opponent is using WATER Monsters.

MRD-118 Bladefly

Card Type:
Effect Monster

Monster Type:
Insect

Attribute:
Wind

Level: 2

ATK: 600

DEF: 700

Rarity: Rare

Use "Bladefly" when your Deck is centered on WIND Monsters. "Bladefly's" effect also affects itself, so this card's ATK is already 500 points higher.

MRD-119 Lady of Faith

Card Type:
Normal Monster

Monster Type:
Spellcaster

Attribute:
Light

Level: 3

ATK: 100

DEF: 800

Rarity: Common

This virtuous monk endured rigorous training, dislikes feuds, and calms our restless souls with her mystical incantations.

MRD-120 Twin-Headed Thunder Dragon

Card Type:
Fusion Monster

Monster Type:
Thunder

Attribute:
Light

Level: 7

ATK: 2800

DEF: 2100

Rarity: Super Rare

Not only is it very easy to create this card by fusing two "Thunder Dragons," but it is quite a force in battle.

MRD-121 Witch's Apprentice

Card Type:
Effect Monster

Monster Type:
Spellcaster

Attribute:
Dark

Level: 2

ATK: 550

DEF: 500

Rarity: Rare

Notice that this card can decrease the ATK of all LIGHT Monsters. It's now possible to destroy your opponent's "Blue-Eyes White Dragon" with your "Summoned Skull!"

MRD-122 Blue-Winged Crown

Card Type:
Normal Monster

Monster Type:
Winged Beast

Attribute:
Wind

Level: 4

ATK: 1600

DEF: 1200

Rarity: Common

"Blue-Winged Crown's" body burns in bluish white flames while its head is crowned with red hot fire. Spend any time admiring its beauty and it'll instantly transform you into ash!

MRD-123 Skull Knight

Card Type:
Fusion Monster

Monster Type:
Spellcaster

Attribute:
Dark

Level: 7

ATK: 2650

DEF: 2250

Rarity: Common

Create "Skull Knight" by fusing "Tainted Wisdom" with "Ancient Brain." Clad in bone armor, this guardian of the underworld's weapon attacks is as impressive as its magical powers.

MRD-124 Gazelle the King of Mythical Beasts

Card Type:
Normal Monster

Monster Type:
Beast

Attribute:
Earth

Level: 4

ATK: 1500

DEF: 1200

Rarity: Common

On its own, this Monster has no extra abilities.

MRD-125 Garnecia Elefantis

Card Type:
Normal Monster

Monster Type:
Beast-Warrior

Attribute:
Earth

Level: 7

ATK: 2400

DEF: 2000

Rarity: Super Rare

This divine servant from the Southern land, "Garnecia Elefantis" is usually calm, but when it gets rowdy, it is impossible to control.

MRD-126 Barrel Dragon

Card Type:
Effect Monster

Monster Type:
Machine

Attribute:
Dark

Level: 7

ATK: 2600

DEF: 2200

Rarity: Ultra Rare

Bandit Keith punished Joey with this card. It's not risky to play heads or tails because there is no negative effect if you lose. On top of that, "Barrel Dragon" can attack. When "Barrel Dragon" is on the Field, use its effect and give your opponent a lot of pressure!

MRD-127 Solemn Judgment

Card Type: **Trap**
Monster Type: —
Attribute: **Trap**
Level: —
ATK: —
DEF: —
Rarity: **Ultra Rare**

You'll get yourself into a bind if you don't use "Solemn Judgment" wisely. This card is more beneficial when your Life Points are low because you'll have less Life Points to lose. Definitely use "Solemn Judgment" when you know negating your opponent's card will guarantee victory.

MRD-128 Magic Jammer

Card Type: **Trap**
Monster Type: —
Attribute: **Trap**
Level: —
ATK: —
DEF: —
Rarity: **Ultra Rare**

Once you Set "Magic Jammer," make sure to have one card that you are willing to discard in your hand. Try not to use "Magic Jammer" until your opponent activates a Spell Card that can seriously cripple you.

MRD-129 Seven Tools of the Bandit

Card Type: **Trap**
Monster Type: —
Attribute: **Trap**
Level: —
ATK: —
DEF: —
Rarity: **Ultra Rare**

Trap Cards can be important cards in your opponent's combo or can seriously damage your strategy. Therefore, paying 1000 Life Points isn't a big deal in comparison!

MRD-130 Horn of Heaven

Card Type: **Trap**
Monster Type: —
Attribute: **Trap**
Level: —
ATK: —
DEF: —
Rarity: **Ultra Rare**

You can negate the Summon and destroy your opponent's Monster no matter how powerful it is. Also notice that you can destroy an Effect Monster without triggering its effect. However, you cannot use "Horn of Heaven" against Fusion and Ritual Monsters.

MRD-131 Shield & Sword

Card Type: **Spell**
Monster Type: —
Attribute: **Spell**
Level: —
ATK: —
DEF: —
Rarity: **Rare**

Line up Level 4 Monsters with 2000 DEF and use "Shield & Sword" to flip ATK and DEF. This simple combo inflicts significant damage to your opponent!

MRD-132 Sword of Deep-Seated

Card Type: **Spell**
Monster Type: —
Attribute: **Spell**
Level: —
ATK: —
DEF: —
Rarity: **Common**

It's great that "Sword of Deep-Seated" raises both ATK and DEF, but if you use it too much, you will only be able to draw this card. Think carefully when using this card.

MRD-133 Block Attack

Card Type: **Spell**
Monster Type: —
Attribute: **Spell**
Level: —
ATK: —
DEF: —
Rarity: **Common**

Use it wisely and you can even destroy the most powerful Monsters with your weakest Monsters. For example, "Summoned Skull" is usually a difficult Monster to destroy. However, with "Block Attack," a weak Monster can easily destroy it when "Summoned Skull" is in Defense Position.

MRD-134 The Unhappy Maiden

Card Type: **Effect Monster**
Monster Type: **Spellcaster**
Attribute: **Light**
Level: **1**
ATK: **0**
DEF: **100**
Rarity: **Common**

With ATK of 0, this card is only useful in face-down Defense Position. However, its effect of ending the Battle Phase is excellent. When your opponent attacks, Setting this Monster using "Ultimate Offering" is best.

MRD-135 Robbin' Goblin

Card Type: **Trap**
Monster Type: —
Attribute: **Trap**
Level: —
ATK: —
DEF: —
Rarity: **Rare**

This card is made for combos. You can use this card with Monsters that can directly attack your opponent, or you can pair it with "White Magical Hat" to make your opponent discard two cards. This card is a real nuisance.

MRD-136 Germ Infection

Card Type: Spell

Monster Type: —

Attribute: Spell

Level: —

ATK: —

DEF: —

Rarity: Common

First use "Swords of Revealing Light" to prevent your opponent from attacking, then attach "Germ Infection" to one of your opponent's Monsters. Three turns later, your opponent's Monster's ATK will have decreased by 900!

MRD-137 Paralyzing Potion

Card Type: Spell

Monster Type: —

Attribute: Spell

Level: —

ATK: —

DEF: —

Rarity: Common

After it is equipped on a Monster, it is difficult to remove. If your opponent Summons a powerful Monster, use "Paralyzing Potion." You now have plenty of time to think of how to destroy your opponent's Monster.

MRD-138 Mirror Force

Card Type: Trap

Monster Type: —

Attribute: Trap

Level: —

ATK: —

DEF: —

Rarity: Ultra Rare

You are limited to only one "Mirror Force" per Deck, but seeing its power, it's easy to understand. The stronger the Monsters your opponent has on his or her Field, the more powerful "Mirror Force's" effect is.

MRD-139 Ring of Magnetism

Card Type: Spell

Monster Type: —

Attribute: Spell

Level: —

ATK: —

DEF: —

Rarity: Common

It's best to equip "Ring of Magnetism" on an Effect Monster Card. For example, if you equip it on "Wall of Illusion," your opponent's Monsters will return to his or her hand.

MRD-140 Share the Pain

Card Type: Spell

Monster Type: —

Attribute: Spell

Level: —

ATK: —

DEF: —

Rarity: Common

When your opponent Summons a powerful Monster, you can use "Share the Pain" to offer it as a Tribute. Also, if you offer "Sangan" or "Witch of the Black Forest" as a Tribute, you can move one card from your deck to your hand.

MRD-141 Stim-Pack

Card Type: Spell

Monster Type: —

Attribute: Spell

Level: —

ATK: —

DEF: —

Rarity: Common

This is a prototype chemical, so the ATK decreases over time. However, for three turns, there is an increase in ATK, so use those three turns wisely!

MRD-142 Heavy Storm

Card Type: Spell

Monster Type: —

Attribute: Spell

Level: —

ATK: —

DEF: —

Rarity: Super Rare

You'll also lose your Spell and Trap Cards, but don't stress out. When your opponent lines up Trap Cards, then use "Heavy Storm" and destroy them all!

MRD-143 Thousand Dragon

Card Type: Fusion Monster

Monster Type: Dragon

Attribute: Wind

Level: 7

ATK: 2400

DEF: 2000

Rarity: Secret Rare

"Thousand Dragon" gather much strength and wisdom through the passage of time. You cannot Summon this Monster until a dragon matures.

MRD-000 Gate Guardian

Card Type: Effect Monster

Monster Type: Warrior

Attribute: Dark

Level: 11

ATK: 3750

DEF: 3400

Rarity: Secret Rare

This Monster used by the Paradox Brothers is incredibly powerful but extremely difficult to Summon.

Magic Ruler

MRL-001 Penguin Knight

Card Type: Effect Monster
Monster Type: Aqua
Attribute: Water
Level: 3
ATK: 900
DEF: 800
Rarity: Common

When Ritual Monsters or Fusion-Material Monsters are sent to the Graveyard, "Penguin Knight" gives you a second chance. This card is a must-have for Exodia Decks! However, it is a little bit difficult to activate this card's effect because there are rare cases when this card is sent directly from your Deck to the Graveyard.

MRL-002 Axe of Despair

Card Type: Spell
Monster Type: —
Attribute: Spell
Level: —
ATK: —
DEF: —
Rarity: Ultra Rare

It's great that you can equip "Axe of Despair" on any Monster. You can also recycle this card. It's fun to equip this card on a Monster that can attack your opponent's Life Points directly.

MRL-003 Black Pendant

Card Type: Spell
Monster Type: —
Attribute: Spell
Level: —
ATK: —
DEF: —
Rarity: Super Rare

This is not the strongest Equip Spell Card, but it's useful for defeating Monsters that are slightly stronger than yours. Even if your Monster is destroyed, there's still a bonus!

MRL-004 Horn of Light

Card Type: Spell
Monster Type: —
Attribute: Spell
Level: —
ATK: —
DEF: —
Rarity: Common

Even if you want to equip "Horn of Light" on a certain Monster, it has to be face-up. This card may be hard to use.

MRL-005 Malevolent Nuzzler

Card Type: Spell
Monster Type: —
Attribute: Spell
Level: —
ATK: —
DEF: —
Rarity: Common

This card is better than "Black Pendant" if you want to use this card over and over. If your Monster's ATK increases by 700, it can destroy Monsters quite a bit stronger than yours.

MRL-006 Spellbinding Circle

Card Type: Trap
Monster Type: —
Attribute: Trap
Level: —
ATK: —
DEF: —
Rarity: Ultra Rare

Not only can you stop your opponent's Monster from attacking, but you can also keep Monsters with Flip Effect from a Flip Summon by keeping them in face-down Defense Position!

MRL-007 Metal Fish

Card Type: Normal Monster
Monster Type: Machine
Attribute: Water
Level: 5
ATK: 1600
DEF: 1900
Rarity: Common

"Metal Fish" is unique because it is a Machine-Type Monster with WATER. Its ATK and DEF are well-balanced, and its 1900 DEF is very desirable.

MRL-008 Electric Snake

Card Type: Effect Monster
Monster Type: Thunder
Attribute: Light
Level: 3
ATK: 800
DEF: 900
Rarity: Common

"Electric Snake" is a good countermeasure against "White Magical Hat," "Robbin' Goblin," and other cards that make you discard cards from your hand.

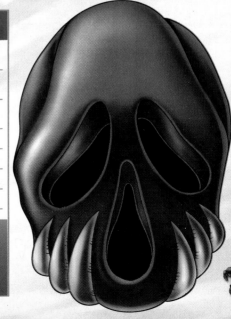

MRL-009 Queen Bird

Card Type: Normal Monster
Monster Type: Winged Beast
Attribute: Wind
Level: 5
ATK: 1200
DEF: 2000
Rarity: Common

"Queen Bird" has surprisingly high DEF for a Winged Beast. It can block most Monsters' attacks although it needs a Tribute Monster to Set.

MRL-010 Ameba

Card Type: Effect Monster
Monster Type: Aqua
Attribute: Water
Level: 1
ATK: 300
DEF: 350
Rarity: Rare

Use this card in the same way as "Griggle." But please remember its effect is NOT activated if it is face-down.

MRL-011 Peacock

Card Type: Normal Monster
Monster Type: Winged Beast
Attribute: Wind
Level: 5
ATK: 1700
DEF: 1500
Rarity: Common

This Winged Beast's main characteristic is its brilliantly beautiful rainbow feathers. The fact that you have to offer another Monster as a Tribute to Summon "Peacock" is a weakness, but it has decent ATK.

MRL-012 Maha Vailo

Card Type: Effect Monster
Monster Type: Spellcaster
Attribute: Light
Level: 4
ATK: 1550
DEF: 1400
Rarity: Super Rare

"Maha Vailo" looks cool, and its effect is just as cool! Construct a Deck that will increase its ATK and DEF quickly.

MRL-013 Guardian of the Throne Room

Card Type: Normal Monster
Monster Type: Machine
Attribute: Light
Level: 4
ATK: 1650
DEF: 1600
Rarity: Common

You can Summon "Guardian of the Throne Room" without offering another Monster as a Tribute. Its LIGHT can come in handy.

MRL-014 Fire Kraken

Card Type: Normal Monster
Monster Type: Aqua
Attribute: Fire
Level: 4
ATK: 1600
DEF: 1500
Rarity: Common

Though "Fire Kraken" is an Aqua-Type Monster, it strangely has FIRE. Its ATK and DEF are both high, so you can count on this card to be useful.

MRL-015 Minar

Card Type: Effect Monster
Monster Type: Insect
Attribute: Earth
Level: 3
ATK: 850
DEF: 750
Rarity: Common

This card is useful against "White Magical Hat" and other cards that make you discard cards from your hand. You can give counter damage in return!

MRL-016 Griggle

Card Type: Effect Monster
Monster Type: Plant
Attribute: Earth
Level: 1
ATK: 350
DEF: 300
Rarity: Common

This card is not just good for "Change of Heart," but it is also effective against "Invader of the Throne." 3000 Life Points will be yours!

MRL-017 Tyhone #2

Card Type:
Normal Monster

Monster Type:
Dragon

Attribute:
Fire

Level: 6

ATK: 1700

DEF: 1900

Rarity: Common

This deep crimson Dragon breathes a burning flame. This is one of the more useful Monsters among FIRE Monsters.

MRL-018 Ancient One of the Deep Forest

Card Type:
Normal Monster

Monster Type:
Beast

Attribute:
Earth

Level: 6

ATK: 1800

DEF: 1900

Rarity: Common

You must offer one Monster as a Tribute to Summon "Ancient One of the Deep Forest," but its 1900 DEF can stop most Monsters. Its ATK of 1800 is also nothing to sneeze at.

MRL-019 Dark Witch

Card Type:
Normal Monster

Monster Type:
Fairy

Attribute:
Light

Level: 5

ATK: 1800

DEF: 1700

Rarity: Common

This is one of the high-class Fairy-Type Monsters with high ATK and DEF.

MRL-020 Weather Report

Card Type:
Effect Monster

Monster Type:
Aqua

Attribute:
Water

Level: 4

ATK: 950

DEF: 1500

Rarity: Common

This is no ordinary snowman! This is a special weapon against "Swords of Revealing Light." Use it and unleash your counterattack!

MRL-021 Mechanical Snail

Card Type:
Normal Monster

Monster Type:
Machine

Attribute:
Dark

Level: 3

ATK: 800

DEF: 1000

Rarity: Common

This looks like a snail with arms and legs, but it is a Machine. Whoever created this robot must be mad.

MRL-022 Giant Turtle Who Feeds on Flames

Card Type:
Normal Monster

Monster Type:
Aqua

Attribute:
Water

Level: 5

ATK: 1400

DEF: 1800

Rarity: Common

This turtle eats flames, but it has WATER. You need to offer another Monster as a Tribute to Summon "Giant Turtle Who Feeds on Flames," but it has decent DEF to defend your Life Points.

MRL-023 Liquid Beast

Card Type:
Normal Monster

Monster Type:
Aqua

Attribute:
Water

Level: 3

ATK: 950

DEF: 800

Rarity: Common

This gross Monster has five eyes and is covered entirely in mud. However, "Liquid Beast" is not as dangerous as it looks.

MRL-024 Hiro's Shadow Scout

Card Type:
Effect Monster

Monster Type:
Fiend

Attribute:
Dark

Level: 2

ATK: 650

DEF: 500

Rarity: Rare

Spell Cards are important in every Deck, especially in setting up combos. By getting rid of your opponent's Spell Cards, you can disrupt his or her strategy.

MRL-025 High Tide Gyojin

Card Type: Normal Monster
Monster Type: Aqua
Attribute: Water
Level: 4
ATK: 1650
DEF: 1300
Rarity: Common

Among Aqua-Type Monsters, "High Tide Gyojin" has decently high ATK and DEF. Having 1650 ATK instead of 1600 is actually a huge difference in battle.

MRL-026 Invader of the Throne

Card Type: Effect Monster
Monster Type: Warrior
Attribute: Earth
Level: 4
ATK: 1350
DEF: 1700
Rarity: Super Rare

Since you cannot use "Invader of the Throne's" effect during the Battle Phase, it's important to know when you should Summon this Monster on to the Field. If you use "Swords of Revealing Light" first, then you can safely Flip Summon this card.

MRL-027 Whiptail Crow

Card Type: Normal Monster
Monster Type: Fiend
Attribute: Dark
Level: 4
ATK: 1650
DEF: 1600
Rarity: Common

"Whiptail Crow" has the same ATK and DEF as "Guardian of the Throne Room," but it has DARK. Therefore, use this card if your Deck is geared toward DARK Monsters.

MRL-028 Slot Machine

Card Type: Normal Monster
Monster Type: Machine
Attribute: Dark
Level: 7
ATK: 2000
DEF: 2300
Rarity: Common

This card cherished by Bandit Keith has high ATK and DEF.

MRL-029 Relinquished

Card Type: Ritual/Effect Monster
Monster Type: Spellcaster
Attribute: Dark
Level: 1
ATK: 0
DEF: 0
Rarity: Ultra Rare

Relinquished is basically a permanent "Change of Heart." Notice that the Monsters that "Relinquished" absorbs become Equip Spell Cards. Try to think how to use this fact to your advantage.

MRL-030 Red Archery Girl

Card Type: Normal Monster
Monster Type: Aqua
Attribute: Water
Level: 4
ATK: 1400
DEF: 1500
Rarity: Common

Pegasus punished Yugi with "Red Archery Girl." Its abilities are average, but if you take her lightly, you'd be in bigger trouble than Yugi.

MRL-031 Gravekeeper's Servant

Card Type: Spell
Monster Type: —
Attribute: Spell
Level: —
ATK: —
DEF: —
Rarity: Common

This is a Continuous Spell Card, so it can prove to be a serious nuisance for your opponent. If you are playing an opponent who relies on combos, he or she will be worried about losing the necessary cards to the Graveyard, so your opponent may stop attacking.

MRL-032 Curse of Fiend

Card Type: Spell
Monster Type: —
Attribute: Spell
Level: —
ATK: —
DEF: —
Rarity: Common

This card is best used to switch your opponent's Monsters from Attack Position to Defense Position. Even if your opponent's Monster has high ATK, it usually has low DEF, which makes it easy to destroy. You can also use this card to switch face-down Defense Position Monsters to face-up Attack Position.

MRL-033 Upstart Goblin

Card Type: Spell
Monster Type: —
Attribute: Spell
Level: —
ATK: —
DEF: —
Rarity: Common

You must decide if drawing one card is worth giving your opponent 1000 Life Points. Test this card out firsthand to learn when to use this card.

Card Catalog

MRL-034 Toll

Card Type: Spell
Monster Type: —
Attribute: Spell
Level: —
ATK: —
DEF: —
Rarity: Common

Since you will also have to pay Life Points in order to attack, it's best to use this card when you have more Life Points than your opponent. If you use this card incorrectly, it can come back and destroy you.

MRL-035 Final Destiny

Card Type: Spell
Monster Type: —
Attribute: Spell
Level: —
ATK: —
DEF: —
Rarity: Common

When using this Spell Card, you have to be careful that your opponent doesn't counter it. If you lose all the cards in your hand and "Final Destiny" is countered, you're in terrible shape. This card is incredibly risky.

MRL-036 Snatch Steal

Card Type: Spell
Monster Type: —
Attribute: Spell
Level: —
ATK: —
DEF: —
Rarity: Ultra Rare

Letting your opponent gain 1000 Life Points every turn may be harsh, but if you immediately offer the Monster you took as a Tribute, then you're at an advantage because your opponent will not gain any Life Points. Think of this card as getting another "Change of Heart!"

MRL-037 Chorus of Sanctuary

Card Type: Spell
Monster Type: —
Attribute: Spell
Level: —
ATK: —
DEF: —
Rarity: Common

"Chorus of Sanctuary" makes it difficult for your opponent to damage your Life Points when the defending Monsters are stronger. Your opponent will also be more wary to attack your face-down Defense Position Monsters.

MRL-038 Confiscation

Card Type: Spell
Monster Type: —
Attribute: Spell
Level: —
ATK: —
DEF: —
Rarity: Super Rare

Paying 1000 Life Points is a pain, but it's great to be able to see your opponent's hand and select one card to discard. If your opponent draws "Witch of the Black Forest" or "Sangan," you can get rid of those annoying cards with "Confiscation."

MRL-039 Delinquent Duo

Card Type: Spell
Monster Type: —
Attribute: Spell
Level: —
ATK: —
DEF: —
Rarity: Ultra Rare

You must pay 1000 Life Points, like "Confiscation," but your opponent has to discard two cards. Though you can't choose which card your opponent has to discard, losing two cards will hurt your opponent.

MRL-040 Darkness Approaches

Card Type: Spell
Monster Type: —
Attribute: Spell
Level: —
ATK: —
DEF: —
Rarity: Common

This Spell Card is made for Effect Monsters. Include Darkness Approaches if your Deck contains many Flip Effect Monsters. You'll be able to use "Magician of Faith's" effect twice!

MRL-041 Fairy's Hand Mirror

Card Type: Trap
Monster Type: —
Attribute: Trap
Level: —
ATK: —
DEF: —
Rarity: Common

The greatest joy turns into the greatest pain. Your opponent will now be worried about using other Spell Cards. The only sure bet is to use Spell Cards when there is only one Monster on the Field.

MRL-042 Tailor of the Fickle

Card Type: Spell
Monster Type: —
Attribute: Spell
Level: —
ATK: —
DEF: —
Rarity: Common

This card is used to counter Equip Spell Cards. Not only does your opponent lose a Spell Card, but you also gain it. Your opponent will be worried about using other Equip Spell Cards.

MRL-043 Rush Recklessly

Card Type: Spell
Monster Type: —
Attribute: Spell
Level: —
ATK: —
DEF: —
Rarity: Rare

Your opponent may think his or her Monster's destroying one of your weak Monsters, but with this Spell Card, your opponent's in for a surprise! Your opponent will worry about attacking if his or her Monster's ATK is only 700 more than yours.

MRL-044 The Reliable Guardian

Card Type: Spell
Monster Type: —
Attribute: Spell
Level: —
ATK: —
DEF: —
Rarity: Common

Similar to "Rush Recklessly," "The Reliable Guardian" is a Quick-Play Spell Card and can be used during your opponent's Battle Phase. You can use this to protect Flip Effect Monsters that you do not want destroyed.

MRL-045 The Forceful Sentry

Card Type: Spell
Monster Type: —
Attribute: Spell
Level: —
ATK: —
DEF: —
Rarity: Ultra Rare

Not only can you see your opponent's hand, you can also get rid of your opponent's most problematic card out of his or her hand without any cost to you. This card has the power to change the tide of battle.

MRL-046 Chain Energy

Card Type: Spell
Monster Type: —
Attribute: Spell
Level: —
ATK: —
DEF: —
Rarity: Common

This card is punishing because doing anything costs Life Points. If you use "Chain Energy" when your opponent is low on Life Points, then you can almost prevent him or her from doing anything.

MRL-047 Mystical Space Typhoon

Card Type: Spell
Monster Type: —
Attribute: Spell
Level: —
ATK: —
DEF: —
Rarity: Ultra Rare

Unlike "Remove Trap," you can now destroy face-down Trap Cards. To counter against "Mystical Space Typhoon," your opponent may now have to place less-useful Spell Cards on the Field.

MRL-048 Giant Trunade

Card Type: Spell
Monster Type: —
Attribute: Spell
Level: —
ATK: —
DEF: —
Rarity: Super Rare

This card helps against your opponent's Spell and Trap Cards that are hindering your strategy. Also, it can return Spell and Trap Cards regardless of their position.

MRL-049 Painful Choice

Card Type: Spell
Monster Type: —
Attribute: Spell
Level: —
ATK: —
DEF: —
Rarity: Super Rare

It may be good to choose five cards that you want, but it may also be fun to choose five cards that you do not want at all. This is a unique way to think out your Deck.

MRL-050 Snake Fang

Card Type: Trap
Monster Type: —
Attribute: Trap
Level: —
ATK: —
DEF: —
Rarity: Common

If your Monster attacks your opponent's face-down Monster in Defense Position, even if your opponent's Monster has higher DEF than your Monster's ATK, use "Snake Fang" and destroy your opponent's Monster.

MRL-051 Black Illusion Ritual

Card Type: Spell
Monster Type: —
Attribute: Spell
Level: —
ATK: —
DEF: —
Rarity: Super Rare

You need this card to Ritual Summon the Ritual Monster "Relinquished." This card is useless by itself, so make sure to get both cards!

MRL-052 Octoberser

Card Type: Normal Monster
Monster Type: Aqua
Attribute: Water
Level: 5
ATK: 1600
DEF: 1400
Rarity: Common

"Octoberser" has the head of a fish and the legs of an octopus.

MRL-053 Psychic Kappa

Card Type: Normal Monster
Monster Type: Aqua
Attribute: Water
Level: 2
ATK: 400
DEF: 1000
Rarity: Common

This creature protects itself against attacks with its various psychic powers.

MRL-054 Horn of the Unicorn

Card Type: Spell
Monster Type: —
Attribute: Spell
Level: —
ATK: —
DEF: —
Rarity: Rare

Not only can you power up any of your Monsters, but you can also return this card from your Graveyard to your Deck for additional uses!

MRL-055 Labyrinth Wall

Card Type: Normal Monster
Monster Type: Rock
Attribute: Earth
Level: 5
ATK: 0
DEF: 3000
Rarity: Common

A labyrinth without an exit surrounds the area.

MRL-056 Wall Shadow

Card Type: Effect Monster
Monster Type: Warrior
Attribute: Dark
Level: 7
ATK: 1600
DEF: 3000
Rarity: Common

You cannot Special Summon "Wall Shadow" unless "Labyrinth Wall" is equipped with "Magical Labyrinth" and offer it as a Tribute.

MRL-057 Twin Long Rods #2

Card Type: Normal Monster
Monster Type: Aqua
Attribute: Water
Level: 3
ATK: 850
DEF: 700
Rarity: Common

This aquatic Monster swings two tails like whips.

MRL-058 Stone Ogre Grotto

Card Type: Normal Monster
Monster Type: Rock
Attribute: Earth
Level: 5
ATK: 1600
DEF: 1500
Rarity: Common

This giant stone ogre is created by stacks and stacks of boulders.

MRL-059 Magical Labyrinth

Card Type: Spell
Monster Type: —
Attribute: Spell
Level: —
ATK: —
DEF: —
Rarity: Common

You need both "Magical Labyrinth" and "Labyrinth Wall" in order to Special Summon "Wall Shadow."

MRL-060 Eternal Rest

Card Type: Spell
Monster Type: —
Attribute: Spell
Level: —
ATK: —
DEF: —
Rarity: Common

You can destroy all Monsters with Equip Spell Cards.

MRL-061 Megamorph

Card Type: Spell

Monster Type: —

Attribute: Spell

Level: —

ATK: —

DEF: —

Rarity: Ultra Rare

This is a powerful Equip Spell Card. If you have less Life Points than your opponent, equip this card on one of your Monsters. If you have more Life Points than your opponent, equip this card on one of your opponent's Monsters.

MRL-062 Commencement Dance

Card Type: Spell

Monster Type: —

Attribute: Spell

Level: —

ATK: —

DEF: —

Rarity: Common

You need this card to Summon the Ritual Monster "Performance of Sword." This card is useless by itself, so make sure to get both cards!

MRL-063 Hamburger Recipe

Card Type: Spell

Monster Type: —

Attribute: Spell

Level: —

ATK: —

DEF: —

Rarity: Common

You need this card to Summon the Ritual Monster "Hungry Burger." This card is useless by itself, so make sure to get both cards!

MRL-064 House of Adhesive Tape

Card Type: Trap

Monster Type: —

Attribute: Trap

Level: —

ATK: —

DEF: —

Rarity: Common

This Trap Card helps you destroy Monsters with low DEF.

MRL-065 Eatgaboon

Card Type: Trap

Monster Type: —

Attribute: Trap

Level: —

ATK: —

DEF: —

Rarity: Common

Slightly different than "House of Adhesive Tape," this Trap Card lets you destroy Monsters with low ATK.

MRL-066 Turtle Oath

Card Type: Spell

Monster Type: —

Attribute: Spell

Level: —

ATK: —

DEF: —

Rarity: Common

You need this card to Summon the Ritual Monster "Crab Turtle." This card is useless by itself, so make sure to get both cards!

MRL-067 Performance of Sword

Card Type: Ritual Monster

Monster Type: Warrior

Attribute: Earth

Level: 6

ATK: 1950

DEF: 1850

Rarity: Common

In order to Ritual Summon "Performance of Sword," you must have "Commencement Dance" and offer Monsters whose total Level Stars are equal to six or more as a Tribute.

MRL-068 Hungry Burger

Card Type: Ritual Monster

Monster Type: Warrior

Attribute: Dark

Level: 6

ATK: 2000

DEF: 1850

Rarity: Common

In order to Ritual Summon "Hungry Burger," you must have "Hamburger Recipe" and offer Monsters whose total Level Stars are equal to six or more as a Tribute.

MRL-069 Crab Turtle

Card Type: Ritual Monster

Monster Type: Aqua

Attribute: Water

Level: 8

ATK: 2550

DEF: 2500

Rarity: Common

In order to Ritual Summon "Crab Turtle," you must have "Turtle Oath" and offer Monsters whose total Level Stars are equal to 8 or more as a Tribute.

Card Catalog

MRL-070 Ryu-Ran

Card Type: **Normal Monster**
Monster Type: **Dragon**
Attribute: **Fire**
Level: **7**
ATK: **2200**
DEF: **2600**
Rarity: **Common**

This Dragon may wear an egg shell, but you'll be in big trouble if you treat it with kiddie gloves!

MRL-071 Manga Ryu-Ran

Card Type: **Toon Monster**
Monster Type: **Dragon**
Attribute: **Fire**
Level: **7**
ATK: **2200**
DEF: **2600**
Rarity: **Rare**

This Toon lets you attack your opponent directly for 2200 damage to his or her Life Points! However, you must have "Toon World" on your side of the field to Special Summon it.

MRL-072 Toon Mermaid

Card Type: **Toon Monster**
Monster Type: **Aqua**
Attribute: **Water**
Level: **4**
ATK: **1400**
DEF: **1500**
Rarity: **Ultra Rare**

Similar to the other Toons, you can attack your opponent directly. However, you must have "Toon World" on your side of the field to Special Summon it.

MRL-073 Toon Summoned Skull

Card Type: **Toon Monster**
Monster Type: **Fiend**
Attribute: **Dark**
Level: **6**
ATK: **2500**
DEF: **1200**
Rarity: **Ultra Rare**

Similar to the other Toons, you can attack your opponent directly. However, you must have "Toon World" on your side of the field to Special Summon it.

MRL-074 Jigen Bakudan

Card Type: **Effect Monster**
Monster Type: **Pyro**
Attribute: **Fire**
Level: **2**
ATK: **200**
DEF: **1000**
Rarity: **Common**

"Jigen Bakudan" allows you to deal direct damage to your opponent's Life Points. If your opponent's Life Points are low, this can be the finishing blow!

MRL-075 Hyozanryu

Card Type: **Normal Monster**
Monster Type: **Dragon**
Attribute: **Light**
Level: **7**
ATK: **2100**
DEF: **2800**
Rarity: **Rare**

This powerful Dragon is entirely covered in diamonds.

MRL-076 Toon World

Card Type: **Spell**
Monster Type: **—**
Attribute: **Spell**
Level: **—**
ATK: **—**
DEF: **—**
Rarity: **Super Rare**

Though you must pay 1000 Life Points, you are now able to Summon Toon Monsters that can deal Direct Damage to your opponent!

MRL-077 Cyber Jar

Card Type: **Effect Monster**
Monster Type: **Rock**
Attribute: **Dark**
Level: **3**
ATK: **900**
DEF: **900**
Rarity: **Rare**

Not only does this card act like a "Dark Hole," but it also allows you to draw cards from your Deck and Special Summon Monsters onto the Field.

MRL-078 Banisher of the Light

Card Type: **Effect Monster**
Monster Type: **Fairy**
Attribute: **Light**
Level: **3**
ATK: **100**
DEF: **2000**
Rarity: **Super Rare**

This Monster has high defense, but it's main effect is to remove cards from the Duel to prevent your opponent from resurrecting cards from the Graveyard.

TRADING CARD GAME

MRL-079 Giant Rat

Card Type:
Effect Monster

Monster Type:
Beast

Attribute:
Earth

Level: 4

ATK: 1400

DEF: 1450

Rarity: Rare

When "Giant Rat" is destroyed, you can Special Summon another Monster to the Field!

MRL-080 Senju of the Thousand Hands

Card Type:
Effect Monster

Monster Type:
Fairy

Attribute:
Light

Level: 4

ATK: 1400

DEF: 1000

Rarity: Rare

This card allows you to search your Deck for the Ritual Monster Card that you need.

MRL-081 UFO Turtle

Card Type:
Effect Monster

Monster Type:
Machine

Attribute:
Fire

Level: 4

ATK: 1400

DEF: 1200

Rarity: Rare

When "UFO Turtle" is destroyed, you can Special Summon another Monster to the Field!

MRL-082 Flash Assailant

Card Type:
Effect Monster

Monster Type:
Fiend

Attribute:
Dark

Level: 4

ATK: 2000

DEF: 2000

Rarity: Common

Though "Flash Assailant" has high ATK and DEF, it is only useful if you have few to no cards in your hand.

MRL-083 Karate Man

Card Type:
Effect Monster

Monster Type:
Warrior

Attribute:
Earth

Level: 3

ATK: 1000

DEF: 1000

Rarity: Rare

You can double the ATK of "Karate Man" for one turn, but it will be destroyed at the end of the turn. Know when to use this effect. Remember this is NOT a Multi-Trigger Effect.

MRL-084 Dark Zebra

Card Type:
Effect Monster

Monster Type:
Beast

Attribute:
Earth

Level: 4

ATK: 1800

DEF: 400

Rarity: Common

"Dark Zebra" has high ATK but very low DEF. Make sure you have additional Monsters on the Field when you Summon "Dark Zebra."

MRL-085 Giant Germ

Card Type:
Effect Monster

Monster Type:
Fiend

Attribute:
Dark

Level: 2

ATK: 1000

DEF: 100

Rarity: Rare

Not only can you damage your opponent's Life Points directly, you can Special Summon another "Giant Germ" and repeat the process again!

MRL-086 Nimble Momonga

Card Type:
Effect Monster

Monster Type:
Beast

Attribute:
Earth

Level: 2

ATK: 1000

DEF: 100

Rarity: Rare

Not only do you regain Life Points, you can Special Summon another "Nimble Momonga" and repeat the process again!

MRL-087 Spear Cretin

Card Type:
Effect Monster

Monster Type:
Fiend

Attribute:
Dark

Level: 2

ATK: 500

DEF: 500

Rarity: Common

"Spear Cretin" can be very effective if your Graveyard contains a powerful Monster while your opponent has weak or no Monsters in his or her Graveyard.

MRL-088 Shining Angel

Card Type: Effect Monster
Monster Type: Fairy
Attribute: Light
Level: 4
ATK: 1400
DEF: 800
Rarity: Rare

When "Shining Angel" is destroyed, you can Special Summon another Monster to the Field!

MRL-089 Boar Soldier

Card Type: Effect Monster
Monster Type: Beast-Warrior
Attribute: Earth
Level: 4
ATK: 2000
DEF: 500
Rarity: Common

"Boar Soldier" only has high ATK when your opponent has no Monsters on his or her Field, so be sure to Flip Summon this Monster wisely.

MRL-090 Mother Grizzly

Card Type: Effect Monster
Monster Type: Beast-Warrior
Attribute: Water
Level: 4
ATK: 1400
DEF: 1000
Rarity: Rare

When "Mother Grizzly" is destroyed, you can Special Summon another Monster to the Field!

MRL-091 Flying Kamakiri #1

Card Type: Effect Monster
Monster Type: Insect
Attribute: Wind
Level: 4
ATK: 1400
DEF: 900
Rarity: Rare

When "Flying Kamakiri #1" is destroyed, you can Special Summon another Monster to the Field!

MRL-092 Ceremonial Bell

Card Type: Effect Monster
Monster Type: Spellcaster
Attribute: Light
Level: 3
ATK: 0
DEF: 1850
Rarity: Common

You can now see your opponent's hand and learn his or her strategy, but so can your opponent!

MRL-093 Sonic Bird

Card Type: Effect Monster
Monster Type: Winged Beast
Attribute: Wind
Level: 4
ATK: 1400
DEF: 1000
Rarity: Common

This card allows you to search your Deck for the Ritual Spell Card that you need.

MRL-094 Mystic Tomato

Card Type: Effect Monster
Monster Type: Plant
Attribute: Dark
Level: 4
ATK: 1400
DEF: 1100
Rarity: Rare

When "Mystic Tomato" is destroyed, you can Special Summon another Monster to the Field!

MRL-095 Kotodama

Card Type: Effect Monster
Monster Type: Fairy
Attribute: Earth
Level: 3
ATK: 0
DEF: 1600
Rarity: Common

If your opponent is playing many of the same card, "Kotodama" prevents your opponent from Summoning them all to the Field.

MRL-096 Gaia Power

Card Type: Spell
Monster Type: —
Attribute: Spell
Level: —
ATK: —
DEF: —
Rarity: Rare

"Gaia Power" increases the ATK of all EARTH Monsters, but it also decreases the DEF.

MRL-097 Umiiruka

Card Type:
Spell

Monster Type: —

Attribute:
Spell

Level: —

ATK: —

DEF: —

Rarity: Common

"Umiiruka" increases the ATK of all WATER Monsters, but it also decreases the DEF.

MRL-098 Molten Destruction

Card Type:
Spell

Monster Type: —

Attribute:
Spell

Level: —

ATK: —

DEF: —

Rarity: Common

"Molten Destruction" increases the ATK of all FIRE Monsters, but it also decreases the DEF.

MRL-099 Rising Air Current

Card Type:
Spell

Monster Type: —

Attribute:
Spell

Level: —

ATK: —

DEF: —

Rarity: Common

"Rising Air Current" increases the ATK of all WIND Monsters, but it also decreases the DEF.

MRL-100 Luminous Spark

Card Type:
Spell

Monster Type: —

Attribute:
Spell

Level: —

ATK: —

DEF: —

Rarity: Common

"Luminous Spark" increases the ATK of all LIGHT Monsters, but it also decreases the DEF.

MRL-101 Mystic Plasma Zone

Card Type:
Spell

Monster Type: —

Attribute:
Spell

Level: —

ATK: —

DEF: —

Rarity: Common

"Mystic Plasma Zone" increases the ATK of all DARK Monsters, but it also decreases the DEF.

MRL-102 Messenger of Peace

Card Type:
Spell

Monster Type: —

Attribute:
Spell

Level: —

ATK: —

DEF: —

Rarity: Super Rare

This card prevents your opponent's strong Monsters from attacking. This helps in stalling your opponent until you can Summon a strong Monster. "Messenger of Peace" is especially useful in Exodia Decks!

MRL-103 Serpent Night Dragon

Card Type:
Normal Monster

Monster Type:
Dragon

Attribute:
Dark

Level: 7

ATK: 2350

DEF: 2400

Rarity:
Secret Rare

This Dragon prides itself on its extremely high DEF.

MRL-000 Blue-Eyes Toon Dragon

Card Type:
Toon Monster

Monster Type:
Dragon

Attribute:
Light

Level: 8

ATK: 3000

DEF: 2500

Rarity:
Secret Rare

This strongest Toon Monster will deal heavy damage to your opponent's Life Points!

Pharaoh's Servant

PSV-001 Steel Ogre Grotto #2

Card Type: Normal Monster
Monster Type: Machine
Attribute: Earth
Level: 6
ATK: 1900
DEF: 2200
Rarity: Common

This Machine ogre is created out of hard steel and has unbelievable strength.

PSV-002 Three-Headed Geedo

Card Type: Normal Monster
Monster Type: Fiend
Attribute: Dark
Level: 4
ATK: 1200
DEF: 1400
Rarity: Common

This Fiend with three heads has a destructive personality.

PSV-003 Parasite Paracide

Card Type: Effect Monster
Monster Type: Insect
Attribute: Earth
Level: 2
ATK: 500
DEF: 300
Rarity: Super Rare

It's fun to watch your opponent scared to draw his or her next card from the Deck. Also, if "Parasite Paracide" is combined with "Insect Barrier," your opponent's Monsters can't damage your Life Points!

PSV-004 7 Completed

Card Type: Spell
Monster Type: —
Attribute: Spell
Level: —
ATK: —
DEF: —
Rarity: Common

If you play with many Machine-Type Monsters, "7 Completed" will help increase the ATK of your Machine-Type Monsters.

PSV-005 Lightforce Sword

Card Type: Trap
Monster Type: —
Attribute: Trap
Level: —
ATK: —
DEF: —
Rarity: Rare

If you're lucky, "Lightforce Sword" will seal the card your opponent needs for a combo. If your opponent has only one card in his or her hand, then you'll know exactly what you'll hit.

PSV-006 Chain Destruction

Card Type: Trap
Monster Type: —
Attribute: Trap
Level: —
ATK: —
DEF: —
Rarity: Ultra Rare

If you destroy all the Monsters necessary in a combo, then the combo can never take place!

PSV-007 Time Seal

Card Type: Trap
Monster Type: —
Attribute: Trap
Level: —
ATK: —
DEF: —
Rarity: Common

Preventing your opponent from drawing a card limits the number of choices he or she can make. You never know when the next card in your opponent's Deck is the card that can destroy you!

PSV-008 Graverobber

Card Type: Trap
Monster Type: —
Attribute: Trap
Level: —
ATK: —
DEF: —
Rarity: Super Rare

2000 Life Points is a lot to pay, so only use "Graverobber" on a very valuable Spell Card that is in your opponent's Graveyard. Make sure it's a Spell Card that can help you achieve victory!

PSV-009 Gift of The Mystical Elf

Card Type: Trap
Monster Type: —
Attribute: Trap
Level: —
ATK: —
DEF: —
Rarity: Common

The more Monsters there are on the Field, the greater the effect of this card.

PSV-010 The Eye of Truth

Card Type:
Trap

Monster Type: —

Attribute:
Trap

Level: —

ATK: —

DEF: —

Rarity: **Common**

Letting your opponent gain 1000 Life Points every turn may be a high price to pay, but being able to see his or her strategy is well worth the cost.

PSV-011 Dust Tornado

Card Type:
Trap

Monster Type: —

Attribute:
Trap

Level: —

ATK: —

DEF: —

Rarity: **Super Rare**

Not only does your opponent lose a Spell or Trap Card, but you get to Set one of your own! It's a win-win situation!

PSV-012 Call Of The Haunted

Card Type:
Trap

Monster Type: —

Attribute:
Trap

Level: —

ATK: —

DEF: —

Rarity: **Ultra Rare**

Surprise your opponent with this Trap Card to bring back a powerful Monster from your Graveyard! If destroying your Monster once was difficult, think how hard it will be the second time!

PSV-013 Solomon's Lawbook

Card Type:
Trap

Monster Type: —

Attribute:
Trap

Level: —

ATK: —

DEF: —

Rarity: **Common**

Skipping your Standby Phase is useful when you have to pay Life Points during the Standby Phase for cards you are playing.

PSV-014 Earthshaker

Card Type:
Trap

Monster Type: —

Attribute:
Trap

Level: —

ATK: —

DEF: —

Rarity: **Common**

If your opponent plays with only a few different Attribute Monsters, then "Earthshaker" can destroy many Monsters in one swoop.

PSV-015 Enchanted Javelin

Card Type:
Trap

Monster Type: —

Attribute:
Trap

Level: —

ATK: —

DEF: —

Rarity: **Common**

If used correctly, you can negate the damage from even the strongest Monster.

PSV-016 Mirror Wall

Card Type:
Trap

Monster Type: —

Attribute:
Trap

Level: —

ATK: —

DEF: —

Rarity: **Super Rare**

Halving your opponent's Monsters' ATK can instantly turn the tide of battle! If your opponent's Monsters are destroyed, then you don't need to pay 2000 Life Points because you'll no longer need "Mirror Wall."

PSV-017 Gust

Card Type:
Trap

Monster Type: —

Attribute:
Trap

Level: —

ATK: —

DEF: —

Rarity: **Common**

Like an eye for an eye, you can destroy one of your opponent's Spell or Trap Cards.

PSV-018 Driving Snow

Card Type:
Trap

Monster Type: —

Attribute:
Trap

Level: —

ATK: —

DEF: —

Rarity: **Common**

Similar to "Gust," you can destroy your opponent's Spell or Trap Card when your own Trap Card is destroyed.

PSV-019 Armored Glass

Card Type:	Trap
Monster Type:	—
Attribute:	Trap
Level:	—
ATK:	—
DEF:	—
Rarity:	Common

Use this card if your opponent plays with many Equip Spell Cards.

PSV-020 World Suppression

Card Type:	Trap
Monster Type:	—
Attribute:	Trap
Level:	—
ATK:	—
DEF:	—
Rarity:	Common

"World Suppression" stops Field Spell Card's effects, which can be useful depending on the status of the Duel.

PSV-021 Mystic Probe

Card Type:	Trap
Monster Type:	—
Attribute:	Trap
Level:	—
ATK:	—
DEF:	—
Rarity:	Common

Use this card wisely if your opponent plays a Continuous Spell Cards that greatly hinders your strategy.

PSV-022 Metal Detector

Card Type:	Trap
Monster Type:	—
Attribute:	Trap
Level:	—
ATK:	—
DEF:	—
Rarity:	Common

"Metal Detector" can be useful when your opponent has you locked down with Continuous Trap Cards.

PSV-023 Numinous Healer

Card Type:	Trap
Monster Type:	—
Attribute:	Trap
Level:	—
ATK:	—
DEF:	—
Rarity:	Common

The more "Numinous Healer" Cards you have in your Deck, the more useful this card is. This card restores a significant portion of your Life Points!

PSV-024 Appropriate

Card Type:	Trap
Monster Type:	—
Attribute:	Trap
Level:	—
ATK:	—
DEF:	—
Rarity:	Rare

Since many players know the advantage of drawing extra cards, they include cards that allow them to draw cards during their non-Draw Phases. Therefore, "Appropriate" can be quite useful.

PSV-025 Forced Requisition

Card Type:	Trap
Monster Type:	—
Attribute:	Trap
Level:	—
ATK:	—
DEF:	—
Rarity:	Rare

Use "Forced Requisition" if your Deck is geared toward destroying your opponent's hand.

PSV-026 DNA Surgery

Card Type:	Trap
Monster Type:	—
Attribute:	Trap
Level:	—
ATK:	—
DEF:	—
Rarity:	Common

"DNA Surgery" allows you to change all different types that have been on the Field to one specific type.

PSV-027 The Regulation of Tribe

Card Type:	Trap
Monster Type:	—
Attribute:	Trap
Level:	—
ATK:	—
DEF:	—
Rarity:	Common

If your opponent plays with only one or few Monster Types, then "The Regulation of Tribe" severely limits his or her attacking capabilities.

PSV-028 Backup Soldier

Card Type: **Trap**

Monster Type: —

Attribute: **Trap**

Level: —

ATK: —

DEF: —

Rarity: **Super Rare**

You can only return Normal Monsters, Fusion Monsters, and/or Ritual Monsters without effect from your Graveyard to your hand. Exodia Decks must have this card.

PSV-029 Major Riot

Card Type: **Trap**

Monster Type: —

Attribute: **Trap**

Level: —

ATK: —

DEF: —

Rarity: **Common**

Even if your Monsters on the Field are weak, you can now Special Summon more powerful Monsters on to the Field although you cannot Special Summon a high-level Monster nor Special Summon a Monster like "Gate Guardian."

PSV-030 Ceasefire

Card Type: **Trap**

Monster Type: —

Attribute: **Trap**

Level: —

ATK: —

DEF: —

Rarity: **Ultra Rare**

"Ceasefire" prevents your Effect Monsters' effects from triggering. As a bonus, your opponent will also take damage to his or her Life Points!

PSV-031 Light of Intervention

Card Type: **Trap**

Monster Type: —

Attribute: **Trap**

Level: —

ATK: —

DEF: —

Rarity: **Common**

"Light of Intervention" prevents Flip Effect Monsters' effects from activating. If used correctly, "Light of Intervention" can stop your opponent's combos.

PSV-032 Respect Play

Card Type: **Trap**

Monster Type: —

Attribute: **Trap**

Level: —

ATK: —

DEF: —

Rarity: **Common**

Though this card signifies fair play, how fair is it see each other's strategies....

PSV-033 Magical Hats

Card Type: **Trap**

Monster Type: —

Attribute: **Trap**

Level: —

ATK: —

DEF: —

Rarity: **Super Rare**

If you have a particular Monster that you want to protect, play "Magical Hats," and the odds are on your side!

PSV-034 Nobleman of Crossout

Card Type: **Spell**

Monster Type: —

Attribute: **Spell**

Level: —

ATK: —

DEF: —

Rarity: **Super Rare**

"Nobleman of Crossout" may remove a particularly dangerous Monster from the Duel. If the Monster is part of your opponent's combo, then your opponent's strategy is destroyed!

PSV-035 Nobleman of Extermination

Card Type: **Spell**

Monster Type: —

Attribute: **Spell**

Level: —

ATK: —

DEF: —

Rarity: **Rare**

Not only can you destroy one of your opponent's Spell and Trap Cards, but if you're lucky, you may remove a particularly nasty Trap Card from the Duel!

PSV-036 The Shallow Grave

Card Type: **Spell**

Monster Type: —

Attribute: **Spell**

Level: —

ATK: —

DEF: —

Rarity: **Rare**

"The Shallow Grave" is especially useful if you have a powerful Monster in your Graveyard while your opponent has weak Monsters in his or her Graveyard.

PSV-037 Premature Burial

Card Type: Spell
Monster Type: —
Attribute: Spell
Level: —
ATK: —
DEF: —
Rarity: Ultra Rare

Though this card is not as powerful as "Monster Reborn," it is another way to retrieve powerful Monsters from your Graveyard.

PSV-038 Inspection

Card Type: Spell
Monster Type: —
Attribute: Spell
Level: —
ATK: —
DEF: —
Rarity: Common

You can learn your opponent's strategy if you know what cards he or she is playing, but be careful not to run out of Life Points!

PSV-039 Prohibition

Card Type: Spell
Monster Type: —
Attribute: Spell
Level: —
ATK: —
DEF: —
Rarity: Rare

If your opponent plays with many of the same Monsters, "Prohibition" can limit his or her selection.

PSV-040 Morphing Jar #2

Card Type: Effect Monster
Monster Type: Rock
Attribute: Earth
Level: 3
ATK: 800
DEF: 700
Rarity: Rare

"Morphing Jar #2" is useful in various situations. If your opponent has powerful Monsters and you have weak Monsters on the Field, then "Morphing Jar" will act like a "Dark Hole" and return all the Monsters to the Decks. It will also allow you to Summon new Monsters on the Field that may be more useful. Also, if your opponent has few Monster Cards in his or her Deck and many Spell and Trap Cards, then your opponent will probably discard many Spell and Trap Cards into the Graveyard before he or she runs across a Monster Card.

PSV-041 Flame Champion

Card Type: Normal Monster
Monster Type: Pyro
Attribute: Fire
Level: 5
ATK: 1900
DEF: 1300
Rarity: Common

This Warrior blocks all attacks with a flame shield.

PSV-042 Twin-Headed Fire Dragon

Card Type: Normal Monster
Monster Type: Pyro
Attribute: Fire
Level: 6
ATK: 2200
DEF: 1700
Rarity: Common

Born in space, this Dragon is actually twin Dragons sharing the same body.

PSV-043 Darkfire Soldier #1

Card Type: Normal Monster
Monster Type: Pyro
Attribute: Fire
Level: 4
ATK: 1700
DEF: 1150
Rarity: Common

This burning soldier is an expert in explosives.

PSV-044 Mr. Volcano

Card Type: Normal Monster
Monster Type: Pyro
Attribute: Fire
Level: 5
ATK: 2100
DEF: 1300
Rarity: Common

This flame wielder is usually calm, but he is very scary when angry.

PSV-045 Darkfire Soldier #2

Card Type:
Normal Monster

Monster Type:
Pyro

Attribute:
Fire

Level: 4

ATK: 1700

DEF: 1000

Rarity: Common

This swordsman learned to harness flames after he fell into a volcano.

PSV-046 Kiseitai

Card Type:
Effect Monster

Monster Type:
Fiend

Attribute:
Dark

Level: 2

ATK: 300

DEF: 800

Rarity: Common

If this card is played face-down in Defense Position, your opponent will most likely attack "Kiseitai" with his or her most powerful Monster. That means you'll gain many Life Points every turn!

PSV-047 Cyber Falcon

Card Type:
Normal Monster

Monster Type:
Machine

Attribute:
Wind

Level: 4

ATK: 1400

DEF: 1200

Rarity: Common

This eagle flies at the speed of sound, thanks to its jet engines.

PSV-048 Flying Kamakiri #2

Card Type:
Normal Monster

Monster Type:
Insect

Attribute:
Wind

Level: 4

ATK: 1500

DEF: 800

Rarity: Common

This flying preying mantis' favorite food is insects.

PSV-049 Harpie's Brother

Card Type:
Normal Monster

Monster Type:
Winged Beast

Attribute:
Wind

Level: 4

ATK: 1800

DEF: 600

Rarity: Common

This birdman flies at incredible speed and can see into great distances with eyes more perceptive than an eagle's.

PSV-050 Buster Blader

Card Type:
Effect Monster

Monster Type:
Warrior

Attribute:
Earth

Level: 7

ATK: 2600

DEF: 2300

Rarity: Ultra Rare

If your opponent plays with many Dragon-Type Monsters, then "Buster Blader" is a must-have for your Deck.

PSV-051 Michizure

Card Type:
Trap

Monster Type: —

Attribute:
Trap

Level: —

ATK: —

DEF: —

Rarity: Rare

"Michizure" is an effective way of getting rid of your opponent's Monsters on the Field. Your Monster may have been destroyed, but so has your opponent's Monster!

PSV-052 Minor Goblin Official

Card Type:
Trap

Monster Type: —

Attribute:
Trap

Level: —

ATK: —

DEF: —

Rarity: Common

"Minor Goblin Official" helps speed up your opponent's demise.

PSV-053 Gamble

Card Type:
Trap

Monster Type: —

Attribute:
Trap

Level: —

ATK: —

DEF: —

Rarity: Common

Like the card name itself, this card is a gamble. If you win, you will draw much-needed cards that can turn the tide of battle. However, if you lose, you lose an important turn.

PSV-054 Attack and Receive

Card Type:
Trap

Monster Type: —

Attribute:
Trap

Level: —

ATK: —

DEF: —

Rarity: **Common**

If you play with "Attack and Receive," try to have three in your Deck. Your opponent will second guess whether to attack you again.

PSV-055 Solemn Wishes

Card Type:
Trap

Monster Type: —

Attribute:
Trap

Level: —

ATK: —

DEF: —

Rarity: **Common**

"Solemn Wishes" helps you regain a lot of Life Points because it is a Continuous Trap Card and stays on the Field.

PSV-056 Skull Invitation

Card Type:
Trap

Monster Type: —

Attribute:
Trap

Level: —

ATK: —

DEF: —

Rarity: **Rare**

This card works great in Decks that force your opponent to discard cards. Also, if your opponent is low on Life Points, he or she will have a hard time playing any card for fear that it will be destroyed.

PSV-057 Bubonic Vermin

Card Type:
Effect Monster

Monster Type:
Beast

Attribute:
Earth

Level: **3**

ATK: **900**

DEF: **600**

Rarity: **Common**

If you have one "Bubonic Vermin," you can soon fill your Field with many "Bubonic Vermin." Find a way to use these creatures to your advantage, such as offering them as a Tribute, because on their own, their low ATK and DEF are not very helpful.

PSV-058 Dark Bat

Card Type:
Normal Monster

Monster Type:
Winged Beast

Attribute:
Wind

Level: **3**

ATK: **1000**

DEF: **1000**

Rarity: **Common**

These bats search for their prey using sonar.

PSV-059 Oni Tank T-34

Card Type:
Normal Monster

Monster Type:
Machine

Attribute:
Earth

Level: **4**

ATK: **1400**

DEF: **1700**

Rarity: **Common**

This tank is possessed by the spirit of a fiend and chases after its enemies.

PSV-060 Overdrive

Card Type:
Normal Monster

Monster Type:
Machine

Attribute:
Earth

Level: **4**

ATK: **1600**

DEF: **1500**

Rarity: **Common**

"Overdrive" is an armored buggy that can drive over any rough terrain.

PSV-061 Burning Land

Card Type:
Spell

Monster Type: —

Attribute:
Spell

Level: —

ATK: —

DEF: —

Rarity: **Common**

If your opponent's Life Points are lower than yours, "Burning Land" can help you speed up your opponent's demise.

PSV-062 Cold Wave

Card Type:
Spell

Monster Type: —

Attribute:
Spell

Level: —

ATK: —

DEF: —

Rarity: **Common**

Use "Cold Wave" to make sure your opponent cannot interfere with your strategy this turn.

PSV-063 Fairy Meteor Crush

Card Type:
Spell

Monster Type: —

Attribute:
Spell

Level: —

ATK: —

DEF: —

Rarity: Super Rare

"Fairy Meteor Crush" gives the same effect as "Mad Sword Beast" to any Monster. Equip this card on a powerful Monster and attack!

PSV-064 Limiter Removal

Card Type:
Spell

Monster Type: —

Attribute:
Spell

Level: —

ATK: —

DEF: —

Rarity: Super Rare

"Limiter Removal" is very effective in Machine-Type Decks to unleash the final blow to your opponent.

PSV-065 Rain of Mercy

Card Type:
Spell

Monster Type: —

Attribute:
Spell

Level: —

ATK: —

DEF: —

Rarity: Common

Use this card wisely because it benefits your opponent as much as it benefits you.

PSV-066 Monster Recovery

Card Type:
Spell

Monster Type: —

Attribute:
Spell

Level: —

ATK: —

DEF: —

Rarity: Rare

If you do not have any useful cards in your hand, use "Monster Recovery" to draw a fresh hand. Also, if you retrieve an Effect Monster Card, you can use its effect again.

PSV-067 Shift

Card Type:
Trap

Monster Type: —

Attribute:
Trap

Level: —

ATK: —

DEF: —

Rarity: Rare

Make sure you have another Monster on the Field than the Monster you're trying to protect, or this card is useless.

PSV-068 Insect Imitation

Card Type:
Spell

Monster Type: —

Attribute:
Spell

Level: —

ATK: —

DEF: —

Rarity: Common

Only use this card if you play with many Insect-Type Monsters in your Deck.

PSV-069 Dimensionhole

Card Type:
Spell

Monster Type: —

Attribute:
Spell

Level: —

ATK: —

DEF: —

Rarity: Rare

If you play "Dimensionhole" followed by "Dark Hole," your Monster will return next turn while your opponent's Monsters are destroyed!

PSV-070 Ground Collapse

Card Type:
Spell

Monster Type: —

Attribute:
Spell

Level: —

ATK: —

DEF: —

Rarity: Common

As long as "Ground Collapse" is on the Field, you can limit the number of Monsters your opponent can Summon to the Field. If you have two "Ground Collapses," your opponent can only have one Monster on the Field!

PSV-071 Magic Drain

Card Type:
Trap

Monster Type: —

Attribute:
Trap

Level: —

ATK: —

DEF: —

Rarity: Rare

"Magic Drain" can either negate your opponent's Spell Card or force him or her to lose an additional Spell Card. Whichever your opponent chooses, it's a bonus for you!

PSV-072 Infinite Dismissal

Card Type: Trap
Monster Type: —
Attribute: Trap
Level: —
ATK: —
DEF: —
Rarity: Common

Many low-level Monsters make up for their lack of ATK and DEF with potent effects. However, "Infinite Dismissal" will destroy these Monsters. You can lockdown your opponent if you use "Infinite Dismissal" in combination with "Gravity Bind."

PSV-073 Gravity Bind

Card Type: Trap
Monster Type: —
Attribute: Trap
Level: —
ATK: —
DEF: —
Rarity: Rare

"Gravity Bind" will stop all your opponent's Monsters cold! If you play many low-level Monsters, "Gravity Bind" will not affect you at all. This card also helps stall your opponent if you're playing an Exodia Deck.

PSV-074 Type Zero Magic Crusher

Card Type: Trap
Monster Type: —
Attribute: Trap
Level: —
ATK: —
DEF: —
Rarity: Common

Play this card if you play with many Spell Cards or if you have useless Spell Cards in your hand when your opponent is low in Life Points.

PSV-075 Shadow of Eyes

Card Type: Trap
Monster Type: —
Attribute: Trap
Level: —
ATK: —
DEF: —
Rarity: Common

"Shadow of Eyes" not only makes your opponent's Flip Effect not activated, but it forces them into Attack Position for your Monsters to destroy!

PSV-076 The Legendary Fisherman

Card Type: Effect Monster
Monster Type: Warrior
Attribute: Water
Level: 5
ATK: 1850
DEF: 1600
Rarity: Ultra Rare

Definitely play "The Legendary Fisherman" if you play "Umi" along with your Sea Serpent, Fish, Thunder, and Aqua-Type Monsters. "The Legendary Fisherman" is protected against Spell Cards and your opponent's Monsters, making it nearly invincible!

PSV-077 Sword Hunter

Card Type: Effect Monster
Monster Type: Warrior
Attribute: Earth
Level: 7
ATK: 2450
DEF: 1700
Rarity: Common

The more Monsters "Sword Hunter" destroys, the stronger "Sword Hunter" gets, making it even harder for your opponent to defeat him!

PSV-078 Drill Bug

Card Type: Effect Monster
Monster Type: Insect
Attribute: Earth
Level: 2
ATK: 1000
DEF: 200
Rarity: Common

If you're playing with "Parasite Paracide," make sure to include "Drill Bug" in your Deck to Summon "Parasite Paracide" quicker.

PSV-079 Deepsea Warrior

Card Type: Effect Monster
Monster Type: Warrior
Attribute: Water
Level: 5
ATK: 1600
DEF: 1800
Rarity: Common

"Deepsea Warrior" works well with "The Legendary Fisherman" since both are unaffected by your opponent's Spell Card.

PSV-080 Bite Shoes

Card Type: Effect Monster
Monster Type: Fiend
Attribute: Dark
Level: 2
ATK: 500
DEF: 300
Rarity: Common

Many Monsters with high ATK have low DEF, so your opponent is in for a surprise when you switch his or her Monster to Defense Position and destroy it!

TRADING CARD GAME

PSV-081 Spikebot

Card Type: Normal Monster

Monster Type: Machine

Attribute: Dark

Level: 5

ATK: 1800

DEF: 1700

Rarity: Common

"Spikebot" swings its spiked balls on its arms wildly, striking both friend and foe.

PSV-082 Invitation to a Dark Sleep

Card Type: Effect Monster

Monster Type: Spellcaster

Attribute: Dark

Level: 5

ATK: 1500

DEF: 1800

Rarity: Common

If your opponent has a powerful Monster on the Field, "Invitation to a Dark Sleep" prevents it from attacking. This will give you additional time to figure out a way to defeat it.

PSV-083 Thousand-Eyes Idol

Card Type: Normal Monster

Monster Type: Spellcaster

Attribute: Dark

Level: 1

ATK: 0

DEF: 0

Rarity: Common

This Spellcaster's ATK and DEF look absolutely useless, but when fused with "Relinquished," you can Summon the mighty "Thousand-Eyes Restrict!"

PSV-084 Thousand-Eyes Restrict

Card Type: Fusion/Effect Monster

Monster Type: Spellcaster

Attribute: Dark

Level: 1

ATK: 0

DEF: 0

Rarity: Ultra Rare

Create "Thousand-Eyes Restrict" by fusing "Thousand-Eyes Idol" and "Relinquished" using "Polymerization." Not only can you absorb your opponent's Monsters, your opponent can no longer attack!

PSV-085 Girochin Kuwagata

Card Type: Normal Monster

Monster Type: Insect

Attribute: Wind

Level: 4

ATK: 1700

DEF: 1000

Rarity: Common

This Insect is only about the size of your thumb, but it can cut through steel.

PSV-086 Hayabusa Knight

Card Type: Effect Monster

Monster Type: Warrior

Attribute: Earth

Level: 3

ATK: 1000

DEF: 700

Rarity: Rare

"Hayabusa Knight" can attack twice, but it has low ATK. However, if you power up "Hayabusa Knight," then attacking twice is double the trouble for your opponent!

PSV-087 Bombardment Beetle

Card Type: Effect Monster

Monster Type: Insect

Attribute: Wind

Level: 2

ATK: 400

DEF: 900

Rarity: Common

Not only can "Bombardment Beetle" help you by destroying an Effect Monster, but you can also see what Monster your opponent is playing.

PSV-088 4-Starred Ladybug of Doom

Card Type: Effect Monster

Monster Type: Insect

Attribute: Wind

Level: 3

ATK: 800

DEF: 1200

Rarity: Common

Since many useful and powerful Monsters are Level 4, "4-Starred Ladybug of Doom" is an effective way to destroy your opponent's Monsters.

PSV-089 Gradius

Card Type: Normal Monster

Monster Type: Machine

Attribute: Light

Level: 4

ATK: 1200

DEF: 800

Rarity: Common

Thanks to its power cells, this high-performance fighter has enhanced abilities.

PSV-090 Red-Moon Baby

Card Type: Effect
Monster Type: Zombie
Attribute: Dark
Level: 3
Attack Points: 700
Defense Points: 1000
Rarity: Rare

"Red-Moon Baby's" effect is very useful, but since it has low ATK and DEF, make sure to power up "Red-Moon Baby" first.

PSV-091 Mad Sword Beast

Card Type: Effect
Monster Type: Dinosaur
Attribute: Earth
Level: 4
Attack Points: 1400
Defense Points: 1200
Rarity: Rare

"Mad Sword Beast" can deal damage to your opponent's Life Points even if your opponent's Monster is in Defense Position! Find ways to power up "Mad Sword Beast" to deal even more damage!

PSV-092 Skull Mariner

Card Type: Normal
Monster Type: Warrior
Attribute: Water
Level: 4
Attack Points: 1600
Defense Points: 900
Rarity: Normal

This pirate ship has a red skull at its front and plunders tourist and cargo ships.

PSV-093 The All-Seeing White Tiger

Card Type: Normal
Monster Type: Beast
Attribute: Wind
Level: 3
Attack Points: 1300
Defense Points: 500
Rarity: Normal

This king of the forest is as feared as it is admired.

PSV-094 Goblin Attack Force

Card Type: Effect
Monster Type: Warrior
Attribute: Earth
Level: 4
Attack Points: 2300
Defense Points: 0
Rarity: Ultra Rare

"Goblin Attack Force" has 2300 ATK, and you do not need to offer another Monster as a Tribute! You can leave this card in Attack Position and not attack to protect your Life Points, or you can attack and deal a lot of damage. But beware; "Goblin Attack Force" will be destroyed on your opponent's next turn if you attack unless you figure out a way to protect it.

PSV-095 Island Turtle

Card Type: Normal
Monster Type: Aqua
Attribute: Water
Level: 4
Attack Points: 1000
Defense Points: 2000
Rarity: Normal

This large turtle is the size of a small island. Trees and animals live on its back because "Island Turtle" never dives underwater.

PSV-096 Wingweaver

Card Type: Normal
Monster Type: Fairy
Attribute: Light
Level: 7
Attack Points: 2750
Defense Points: 2400
Rarity: Normal

"Wingweaver" soars with six wings and brings peace and hope to the world.

PSV-097 Science Soldier

Card Type: Normal

Monster Type: Warrior

Attribute: Dark

Level: 3

Attack Points: 800

Defense Points: 800

Rarity: Normal

"Science Soldier" is the acme of technology and equipped with high-tech weaponry.

PSV-098 Souls of the Forgotten

Card Type: Normal

Monster Type: Fiend

Attribute: Dark

Level: 2

Attack Points: 900

Defense Points: 200

Rarity: Normal

This spirit is an amalgamation of various vengeful souls.

PSV-099 Dokuroyaiba

Card Type: Normal

Monster Type: Fiend

Attribute: Fire

Level: 3

Attack Points: 1000

Defense Points: 400

Rarity: Normal

This boomerang won't stop flying until it strikes its enemy.

PSV-100 The Fiend Megacyber

Card Type: Effect

Monster Type: Warrior

Attribute: Dark

Level: 6

Attack Points: 2200

Defense Points: 1200

Rarity: Ultra Rare

Summoning a Monster with 2200 ATK without having to offer another Monster as a Tribute is incredible! You may want to hold off Summoning your own Monsters until your opponent has two or more than you on the Field.

PSV-101 Gearfried the Iron Knight

Card Type: Effect

Monster Type: Warrior

Attribute: Earth

Level: 4

Attack Points: 1800

Defense Points: 1600

Rarity: Super Rare

"Gearfried the Iron Knight" has high ATK for a Level 4 Monster. Though you can't use Equip Spell Cards on "Gearfried the Iron Knight," neither can your opponent!

PSV-102 Insect Barrier

Card Type: Magic

Monster Type: —

Attribute: Magic

Level: —

Attack Points: —

Defense Points: —

Rarity: Normal

If you combo "Insect Barrier" with "Parasite Paracide," you can prevent your opponent's Monsters from damaging your Life Points.

PSV-103 Beast of Talwar

Card Type: Normal

Monster Type: Fiend

Attribute: Dark

Level: 6

Attack Points: 2400

Defense Points: 2150

Rarity: Ultra Rare

This incredibly powerful Monster has both high ATK and DEF, and you only need to offer one Monster as a Tribute to Summon "Beast of Talwar!"

PSV-104 Imperial Order

Card Type: Trap

Monster Type: —

Attribute: Trap

Level: —

Attack Points: —

Defense Points: —

Rarity: Secret Rare

If you prevent your opponent from using Spell Cards, then you can disrupt his or her combos and strategies. Also, without Spell Cards, your opponent will have a hard time destroying "Imperial Order!"

PSV-000 Jinzo

Card Type: Effect

Monster Type: Machine

Attribute: Dark

Level: 6

Attack Points: 2400

Defense Points: 1500

Rarity: Secret Rare

"Jinzo" prevents Trap Cards from activating, which can seriously cripple your opponent's strategy if he or she relies on Trap Cards.

Labyrinth of Nightmare

LON-001 The Masked Beast

Card Type: Ritual Monster
Monster Type: Fiend
Attribute: Dark
Level: 8
ATK: 3200
DEF: 1800
Rarity: Ultra Rare

This Monster can only be Ritual Summoned with the Ritual Spell Card, "Curse of the Masked Beast." You must also offer Monsters whose total Level Stars equal 8 or more as a Tribute from the Field or your hand.

LON-002 Swordsman of Landstar

Card Type: Normal Monster
Monster Type: Warrior
Attribute: Earth
Level: 3
ATK: 500
DEF: 1200
Rarity: Common

An amateur with a sword, this fairy warrior relies on its mysterious powers.

LON-003 Humanoid Slime

Card Type: Normal Monster
Monster Type: Aqua
Attribute: Water
Level: 4
ATK: 800
DEF: 2000
Rarity: Common

This slime apparently has some human genes in its genetic makeup.

LON-004 Worm Drake

Card Type: Normal Monster
Monster Type: Reptile
Attribute: Earth
Level: 4
ATK: 1400
DEF: 1500
Rarity: Common

Once this Monster wraps itself around a victim, there is no escape.

LON-005 Humanoid Worm Drake

Card Type: Fusion Monster
Monster Type: Aqua
Attribute: Water
Level: 7
ATK: 2200
DEF: 2000
Rarity: Common

"Worm Drake" + "Humanoid Slime"

LON-006 Revival Jam

Card Type: Effect Monster
Monster Type: Aqua
Attribute: Water
Level: 4
ATK: 1500
DEF: 500
Rarity: Super Rare

When this card is sent to the Graveyard as a result of battle, you can Special Summon this card in face-up Defense Position at your next Standby Phase by paying 1000 Life Points. This must be declared when the Monster is destroyed. You cannot change its position during the same turn it is Special Summoned in this way.

LON-007 Flying Fish

Card Type: Normal Monster
Monster Type: Fish
Attribute: Wind
Level: 4
ATK: 800
DEF: 500
Rarity: Common

Three wishes are granted to those fortunate enough to see this Monster in flight.

LON-008 Amphibian Beast

Card Type: Normal Monster
Monster Type: Fish
Attribute: Water
Level: 6
ATK: 2400
DEF: 2000
Rarity: Rare

On land or in the sea, the speed of this Monster is unmatchable.

LON-009 Shining Abyss

Card Type: Normal Monster
Monster Type: Fairy
Attribute: Light
Level: 4
ATK: 1600
DEF: 1800
Rarity: Common

This Monster employs the powers of both LIGHT and DARK.

LON-010 Gadget Soldier

Card Type:
Normal Monster

Monster Type:
Machine

Attribute:
Fire

Level: 6

ATK: 1800

DEF: 2000

Rarity: Common

A rust-free machine warrior born to battle.

LON-011 Grand Tiki Elder

Card Type:
Normal Monster

Monster Type:
Fiend

Attribute:
Dark

Level: 4

ATK: 1500

DEF: 800

Rarity: Common

A masked Monster that wields the most deadly of curses.

LON-012 Melchid the Four-Face Beast

Card Type:
Normal Monster

Monster Type:
Fiend

Attribute:
Dark

Level: 4

ATK: 1500

DEF: 1200

Rarity: Common

This Monster has four different masks for four different attacks.

LON-013 Nuvia the Wicked

Card Type:
Effect Monster

Monster Type:
Fiend

Attribute:
Dark

Level: 4

ATK: 2000

DEF: 800

Rarity: Rare

If this Monster is Summoned by a Normal Summon, it is destroyed. The ATK of this card is decreased by 200 points for each Monster on your opponent's side of the Field.

LON-014 Chosen One

Card Type:
Spell

Monster Type: —

Attribute:
Spell

Level: —

ATK: —

DEF: —

Rarity: Common

Select 1 Monster Card and 2 non-Monster Cards from your hand. Your opponent randomly selects 1 of the 3 cards. If it is the Monster Card, it is immediately Special Summoned in face-up Attack or Defense Position and the remaining 2 cards are sent to the Graveyard. If it is not a Monster Card, all 3 cards are sent to the Graveyard.

LON-015 Mask of Weakness

Card Type:
Trap

Monster Type: —

Attribute:
Trap

Level: —

ATK: —

DEF: —

Rarity: Common

This card can only be activated in the Battle Phase. Select 1 attacking Monster and decrease the selected Monster's ATK by 700 points during the turn this card is activated.

LON-016 Curse of the Masked Beast

Card Type:
Spell

Monster Type: —

Attribute:
Spell

Level: —

ATK: —

DEF: —

Rarity: Common

This card is used to Ritual Summon "The Masked Beast." You must also offer Monsters whose total Level Stars equal 8 or more as a Tribute from the Field or your hand.

LON-017 Mask of Dispel

Card Type:
Spell

Monster Type: —

Attribute:
Spell

Level: —

ATK: —

DEF: —

Rarity: Super Rare

Select 1 face-up Spell Card on the Field. The controller of the Spell Card must take damage of 500 Life Points during each of his/her Standby Phases. When the selected card is destroyed or removed from the Field, this card is also destroyed.

LON-018 Mask of Restrict

Card Type:
Trap

Monster Type: —

Attribute:
Trap

Level: —

ATK: —

DEF: —

Rarity: Ultra Rare

No matter what the situation, neither player can offer any Monster as a Tribute.

LON-019 Mask of the Accursed

Card Type: Spell
Monster Type: —
Attribute: Spell
Level: —
ATK: —
DEF: —
Rarity: Super Rare

The Monster equipped with this card cannot attack. In addition, the player controlling the equipped Monster must take damage of 500 Life Points during each of your Standby Phases.

LON-020 Mask of Brutality

Card Type: Spell
Monster Type: —
Attribute: Spell
Level: —
ATK: —
DEF: —
Rarity: Rare

A Monster equipped with this card increases its ATK by 1000 points and decreases its DEF by 1000 points. Pay 1000 Life Points during each of your Standby Phases. If you cannot, this card is destroyed.

LON-021 Return of the Doomed

Card Type: Spell
Monster Type: —
Attribute: Spell
Level: —
ATK: —
DEF: —
Rarity: Rare

Discard 1 Monster Card from your hand to the Graveyard. Return 1 of your Monsters that is sent to your Graveyard during this turn as a result of battle to your hand at the end of this turn.

LON-022 Lightning Blade

Card Type: Spell
Monster Type: —
Attribute: Spell
Level: —
ATK: —
DEF: —
Rarity: Common

This card can only be equipped to Warrior-Type Monsters. Increases the ATK of the equipped Monster by 800 points and decreases the ATK of all WATER Monsters on the Field by 500 points.

LON-023 Tornado Wall

Card Type: Trap
Monster Type: —
Attribute: Trap
Level: —
ATK: —
DEF: —
Rarity: Common

This card can only be activated when "Umi" is active on the Field. As long as "Umi" remains face-up on the Field, any damage to your Life Points becomes 0. When "Umi" is destroyed or removed from the Field, this card is also destroyed.

LON-024 Fairy Box

Card Type: Trap
Monster Type: —
Attribute: Trap
Level: —
ATK: —
DEF: —
Rarity: Common

Each time a Monster on your opponent's side of the Field attacks, toss a coin and call Heads or Tails. If you call it right, the attacking Monster's ATK becomes 0 only during the Battle Phase. Pay 500 Life Points during each of your Standby Phases. If you cannot, this card is destroyed.

LON-025 Torrential Tribute

Card Type: Trap
Monster Type: —
Attribute: Trap
Level: —
ATK: —
DEF: —
Rarity: Ultra Rare

You can activate this card when a Monster is Summoned (including Flip Summon and Special Summon). Destroy all Monsters on the Field.

LON-026 Jam Breeding Machine

Card Type: Spell
Monster Type: —
Attribute: Spell
Level: —
ATK: —
DEF: —
Rarity: Rare

During each of your Standby Phases, Special Summon 1 "Slime Token" (face-up Attack Position/Aqua-Type/WATER/LEVEL 1/ATK 500/DEF 500) to your side of the Field. As long as this card remains face-up on the Field, you cannot Summon (including Flip Summon and Special Summon) any other Monster.

LON-027 Infinite Cards

Card Type: Spell
Monster Type: —
Attribute: Spell
Level: —
ATK: —
DEF: —
Rarity: Rare

As long as this card remains face-up on the Field, there is no limit to the number of cards in both players' hands.

LON-028 Jam Defender

Card Type: Trap

Monster Type: —

Attribute: Trap

Level: —

ATK: —

DEF: —

Rarity: Common

Each time a Monster on your opponent's side of the Field attacks a Monster on your side of the Field and you have "Revival Jam" face-up on the Field, you can change the attack target to "Revival Jam."

LON-029 Card of Safe Return

Card Type: Spell

Monster Type: —

Attribute: Spell

Level: —

ATK: —

DEF: —

Rarity: Ultra Rare

When a Monster is Special Summoned to the Field from your Graveyard, you can draw 1 card from your Deck.

LON-030 Lady Panther

Card Type: Effect Monster

Monster Type: Beast-Warrior

Attribute: Earth

Level: 4

ATK: 1400

DEF: 1300

Rarity: Common

Offer this face-up card as a Tribute to return 1 of your Monsters destroyed in battle during this turn to the top of your Deck.

LON-031 The Unfriendly Amazon

Card Type: Effect Monster

Monster Type: Warrior

Attribute: Earth

Level: 4

ATK: 2000

DEF: 1000

Rarity: Common

Offer 1 of your Monsters on the Field as a Tribute (excluding this Monster) during each of your Standby Phases. If you cannot, this card is destroyed. Monsters used for a Tribute Summon or that are offered as Tributes due to other cards' effects are excluded.

LON-032 Amazon Archer

Card Type: Effect Monster

Monster Type: Warrior

Attribute: Earth

Level: 4

ATK: 1400

DEF: 1000

Rarity: Common

Offer 2 Monsters on your side of the Field as a Tribute to inflict 1200 points of Direct Damage to your opponent's Life Points. Monsters used for a Tribute Summon or that are offered as Tributes due to other cards' effects are excluded.

LON-033 Crimson Sentry

Card Type: Effect Monster

Monster Type: Warrior

Attribute: Fire

Level: 4

ATK: 1500

DEF: 1200

Rarity: Common

Offer this face-up card as a Tribute to return 1 of your Monsters destroyed in battle during this turn to the bottom of your Deck.

LON-034 Fire Princess

Card Type: Effect Monster

Monster Type: Pyro

Attribute: Fire

Level: 4

ATK: 1300

DEF: 1500

Rarity: Super Rare

Inflict 500 points of Direct Damage to your opponent's Life Points each time you increase your own Life Points.

LON-035 Lady Assailant of Flames

Card Type: Effect Monster

Monster Type: Pyro

Attribute: Fire

Level: 4

ATK: 1500

DEF: 1000

Rarity: Common

FLIP: Remove 3 cards from the top of your Deck from play to inflict 800 points of Direct Damage to your opponent's Life Points.

LON-036 Fire Sorcerer

Card Type: Effect Monster

Monster Type: Spellcaster

Attribute: Fire

Level: 4

ATK: 1000

DEF: 1500

Rarity: Common

FLIP: Randomly select 2 cards from your hand and remove them from play to inflict 800 points of Direct Damage to your opponent's Life Points.

LON-037 Spirit of the Breeze

Card Type: **Effect Monster**

Monster Type: **Fairy**

Attribute: **Wind**

Level: **3**

ATK: **0**

DEF: **1800**

Rarity: **Rare**

As long as this card remains on your side of the Field in face-up Attack Position, increase your Life Points by 1000 points during each of your Standby Phases.

LON-038 Dancing Fairy

Card Type: **Effect Monster**

Monster Type: **Fairy**

Attribute: **Wind**

Level: **4**

ATK: **1700**

DEF: **1000**

Rarity: **Common**

As long as this card remains on your side of the Field in face-up Defense Position, increase your Life Points by 1000 points during each of your Standby Phases.

LON-039 Fairy Guardian

Card Type: **Effect Monster**

Monster Type: **Fairy**

Attribute: **Wind**

Level: **3**

ATK: **1000**

DEF: **1000**

Rarity: **Common**

Offer this face-up card as a Tribute to return 1 Spell Card sent to your Graveyard by your opponent during this turn to the bottom of your Deck.

LON-040 Empress Mantis

Card Type: **—**

Monster Type: **Insect**

Attribute: **Wind**

Level: **6**

ATK: **2200**

DEF: **1400**

Rarity: **Common**

Queen of an army of giant mantises whose command moves legions.

LON-041 Cure Mermaid

Card Type: **Effect Monster**

Monster Type: **Fish**

Attribute: **Water**

Level: **4**

ATK: **1500**

DEF: **800**

Rarity: **Common**

As long as this card remains face-up on your side of the Field, increase your Life Points by 800 points during each of your Standby Phases.

LON-042 Hysteric Fairy

Card Type: **Effect Monster**

Monster Type: **Fairy**

Attribute: **Light**

Level: **4**

ATK: **1800**

DEF: **500**

Rarity: **Common**

Offer 2 Monsters on your side of the Field as a Tribute to increase your Life Points by 1000 points. Monsters used for a Tribute Summon or that are offered as Tributes due to other cards' effects are excluded.

LON-043 Bio-Mage

Card Type: **Normal Monster**

Monster Type: **Fairy**

Attribute: **Light**

Level: **3**

ATK: **1150**

DEF: **1000**

Rarity: **Common**

A mysterious priest created as a result of the latest advances in biotechnology.

LON-044 The Forgiving Maiden

Card Type: **Effect Monster**

Monster Type: **Fairy**

Attribute: **Light**

Level: **4**

ATK: **850**

DEF: **2000**

Rarity: **Common**

Offer this face-up card as a Tribute to return 1 of your Monsters destroyed in battle during this turn to your hand.

LON-045 St. Joan

Card Type: **Fusion Monster**

Monster Type: **Fairy**

Attribute: **Light**

Level: **7**

ATK: **2800**

DEF: **2000**

Rarity: **Common**

"The Forgiving Maiden" + "Marie the Fallen One"

LON-046 Marie the Fallen One

Card Type:
Effect Monster

Monster Type:
Fiend

Attribute:
Dark

Level: 5

ATK: 1700

DEF: 1200

Rarity: Rare

As long as this card exists in your Graveyard, increase your Life Points by 200 points during each of your Standby Phases.

LON-047 Jar of Greed

Card Type:
Trap

Monster Type: —

Attribute:
Trap

Level: —

ATK: —

DEF: —

Rarity: Super Rare

Draw 1 card from your Deck.

LON-048 Scroll of Bewitchment

Card Type:
Spell

Monster Type: —

Attribute:
Spell

Level: —

ATK: —

DEF: —

Rarity: Common

Select 1 Attribute when you activate this card. Change the Attribute of the equipped Monster to the one you select.

LON-049 United We Stand

Card Type:
Spell

Monster Type: —

Attribute:
Spell

Level: —

ATK: —

DEF: —

Rarity: Ultra Rare

For every face-up Monster you control, increase the ATK and DEF of the equipped Monster by 800 points.

LON-050 Mage Power

Card Type:
Spell

Monster Type: —

Attribute:
Spell

Level: —

ATK: —

DEF: —

Rarity: Ultra Rare

For every Spell and Trap Card on your side of the Field, increase the ATK and DEF of the equipped Monster by 500 points.

LON-051 Offerings to the Doomed

Card Type:
Spell

Monster Type: —

Attribute:
Spell

Level: —

ATK: —

DEF: —

Rarity: Common

Destroys 1 face-up Monster. Skip your next Draw Phase.

LON-052 The Portrait's Secret

Card Type:
Normal Monster

Monster Type:
Fiend

Attribute:
Earth

Level: 4

ATK: 1200

DEF: 1500

Rarity: Common

A portrait cursed by the artist, it is said to bring ill fortune to anyone who owns it.

LON-053 The Gross Ghost of Fled Dreams

Card Type:
Normal Monster

Monster Type:
Fiend

Attribute:
Dark

Level: 4

ATK: 1300

DEF: 1800

Rarity: Common

This Monster feeds on the dreams of an unwary sleeper, dragging the victim into eternal slumber.

LON-054 Headless Knight

Card Type:
Normal Monster

Monster Type:
Fiend

Attribute:
Earth

Level: 4

ATK: 1450

DEF: 1700

Rarity: Common

A haunted spirit of a falsely accused knight who wanders in search of truth and justice.

Card Catalog

LON-055 Earthbound Spirit

Card Type: Normal Monster
Monster Type: Fiend
Attribute: Earth
Level: 4
ATK: 500
DEF: 2000
Rarity: Common

A vengeful creature formed by the spirits of fallen warriors, it drags any who dare approach it into the deepest bowels of the earth.

LON-056 The Earl of Demise

Card Type: Normal Monster
Monster Type: Fiend
Attribute: Dark
Level: 5
ATK: 2000
DEF: 700
Rarity: Common

This gentlemanly creature is extremely wicked, feared by man and Fiend alike.

LON-057 Boneheimer

Card Type: Normal Monster
Monster Type: Aqua
Attribute: Water
Level: 3
ATK: 850
DEF: 400
Rarity: Common

This Monster wanders the seas, sucking dry any creatures it may encounter.

LON-058 Flame Dancer

Card Type: Normal Monster
Monster Type: Pyro
Attribute: Fire
Level: 2
ATK: 550
DEF: 450
Rarity: Common

This Monster moves while swinging its burning rope.

LON-059 Spherous Lady

Card Type: Normal Monster
Monster Type: Rock
Attribute: Earth
Level: 3
ATK: 400
DEF: 1400
Rarity: Common

Many have been deceived by the beauty of this vampire.

LON-060 Lightning Conger

Card Type: Normal Monster
Monster Type: Thunder
Attribute: Water
Level: 3
ATK: 350
DEF: 750
Rarity: Common

This massive eel generates huge charges of electricity and unleashes them as thunderbolts.

LON-061 Jowgen the Spiritualist

Card Type: Effect Monster
Monster Type: Spellcaster
Attribute: Light
Level: 3
ATK: 200
DEF: 1300
Rarity: Rare

Randomly discard 1 card from your hand to the Graveyard to destroy all Special Summoned Monsters on the Field. In addition, as long as this card remains face-up on the Field, no Monsters can be Special Summoned.

LON-062 Kycoo the Ghost Destroyer

Card Type: Effect Monster
Monster Type: Spellcaster
Attribute: Dark
Level: 4
ATK: 1800
DEF: 700
Rarity: Super Rare

Each time this card inflicts battle damage to your opponent's Life Points, you can remove up to 2 cards in your opponent's Graveyard from play. In addition, as long as this card remains face-up on the Field, your opponent cannot remove any cards in either Graveyard from play.

LON-063 Summoner of Illusions

Card Type: Effect Monster

Monster Type: Spellcaster

Attribute: Light

Level: 3

ATK: 800

DEF: 900

Rarity: Common

FLIP: Offer 1 Monster on your side of the Field as a Tribute (excluding this Monster). Special Summon 1 Fusion Monster Card from your Fusion Deck. The Fusion Monster is destroyed at the end of the turn this card is activated.

LON-064 Bazoo the Soul-Eater

Card Type: Effect Monster

Monster Type: Beast

Attribute: Earth

Level: 4

ATK: 1600

DEF: 900

Rarity: Super Rare

You can remove up to 3 cards in your Graveyard from play to increase the ATK of this Monster by 300 points for each card removed from play until the end of your opponent's next turn. This effect can only be used once during your turn.

LON-065 Dark Necrofear

Card Type: Effect Monster

Monster Type: Fiend

Attribute: Dark

Level: 8

ATK: 2200

DEF: 2800

Rarity: Ultra Rare

This card can only be Special Summoned by removing 3 Fiend-Type Monsters in your Graveyard from play. When this card is destroyed in battle or by your opponent's card effect, it is treated as an Equip Spell Card at the end of the turn. Equip 1 of your opponent's Monsters with this card. As long as it is equipped with this card, you control the equipped Monster.

LON-066 Soul of Purity and Light

Card Type: Effect Monster

Monster Type: Fairy

Attribute: Light

Level: 6

ATK: 2000

DEF: 1800

Rarity: Common

This card can only be Special Summoned by removing 2 LIGHT Monsters in your Graveyard from play. As long as this card remains face-up on the Field, decrease the ATK of all Monsters on your opponent's side of the Field by 300 points during his/her Battle Phase.

LON-067 Spirit of Flames

Card Type: Effect Monster

Monster Type: Pyro

Attribute: Fire

Level: 4

ATK: 1700

DEF: 1000

Rarity: Common

This card can only be Special Summoned by removing 1 FIRE Monster in your Graveyard from play. Increase the ATK of this Monster by 300 points during your Battle Phase.

LON-068 Aqua Spirit

Card Type: Effect Monster

Monster Type: Aqua

Attribute: Water

Level: 4

ATK: 1600

DEF: 1200

Rarity: Common

This card can only be Special Summoned by removing 1 WATER Monster in your Graveyard from play. As long as this Monster remains face-up on the Field, during each of your opponent's Standby Phases, you can change the battle position of 1 of your opponent's face-up Monster Cards. Once changed, the Monster must remain in this position for the rest of the turn.

LON-069 The Rock Spirit

Card Type: Effect Monster

Monster Type: Rock

Attribute: Earth

Level: 4

ATK: 1700

DEF: 1000

Rarity: Common

This Monster can only be Special Summoned by removing 1 EARTH Monster in your Graveyard from play. Increase the ATK of this Monster by 300 points during your opponent's Battle Phase.

LON-070 Garuda the Wind Spirit

Card Type: Effect Monster

Monster Type: Winged Beast

Attribute: Wind

Level: 4

ATK: 1600

DEF: 1200

Rarity: Common

This Monster can only be Special Summoned by removing 1 WIND Monster in your Graveyard from play. As long as this Monster remains face-up on the Field, you may change the battle position of 1 of your opponent's face-up Monster Cards at each End Phase of your opponent's turn.

Card Catalog

LON-071 Gilasaurus

Card Type: Effect Monster
Monster Type: Winged Beast
Attribute: Earth
Level: 3
ATK: 1400
DEF: 400
Rarity: Rare

You may treat the Normal Summon of this card as a Special Summon. If you select Special Summon, your opponent may select a Monster Card from his/her Graveyard and Special Summon the Monster to the Field.

LON-072 Tornado Bird

Card Type: Effect Monster
Monster Type: Winged Beast
Attribute: Wind
Level: 4
ATK: 1100
DEF: 1000
Rarity: Rare

FLIP: Return 2 Magic or Trap Cards on the Field to the hands of their owner.

LON-073 Dreamsprite

Card Type: Effect Monster
Monster Type: Plant
Attribute: Light
Level: 2
ATK: 300
DEF: 200
Rarity: Common

When attacked by your opponent's Monster, select another 1 of your Monster Cards and designate it as the attack's target, then calculate damage.

LON-074 Zombyra the Dark

Card Type: Effect Monster
Monster Type: Warrior
Attribute: Dark
Level: 4
ATK: 2100
DEF: 500
Rarity: Common

This card cannot attack a player directly. Each time this card destroys a Monster in battle, decrease the ATK of this card by 200 points.

LON-075 Supply

Card Type: Effect Monster
Monster Type: Warrior
Attribute: Earth
Level: 4
ATK: 1300
DEF: 800
Rarity: Common

FLIP: Return 2 Fusion-Material Monsters that were sent to the Graveyard as a result of a Fusion Summon to your hand.

LON-076 Maryokutai

Card Type: Effect Monster
Monster Type: Aqua
Attribute: Water
Level: 3
ATK: 900
DEF: 900
Rarity: Common

The effect of this card can only be applied during your opponent's turn. When your opponent activates a Spell Card, offer this face-up card as a Tribute to negate the activation of the Spell Card and destroy it.

LON-077 The Last Warrior from Another Planet

Card Type: Fusion/Effect Monster
Monster Type: Warrior
Attribute: Earth
Level: —
ATK: 2350
DEF: 2300
Rarity: Ultra Rare

"Zombyra the Dark" + "Maryokutai" When this card is Special Summoned, destroy all Monsters on your side of the Field except this card. As long as this card remains face-up on the Field, both player cannot Summon (including Flip Summon or Special Summon) any Monster.

LON-078 Collected Power

Card Type: Trap
Monster Type: —
Attribute: Trap
Level: —
ATK: —
DEF: —
Rarity: Common

Select 1 face-up Monster on the Field. Equip this Monster with all face-up Equip Spell Cards on the Field. If the target of the Equip Spell Card is not correct, destroy the Equip Spell Card.

LON-079 Dark Spirit of the Silent

Card Type: Trap
Monster Type: —
Attribute: Trap
Level: —
ATK: —
DEF: —
Rarity: Super Rare

This card can only be activated during your opponent's Battle Step. Negate the attack of 1 Monster and select another 1 of your opponent's face-up Monsters and have it attack. If the new targeted attacking Monster is in face-up Defense Position, change it to Attack Position.

LON-080 Royal Command

Card Type:
Trap

Monster Type: —

Attribute:
Trap

Level: —

ATK: —

DEF: —

Rarity: Ultra Rare

Negates the activation and effects of all Flip Effect Monsters.

LON-081 Riryoku Field

Card Type:
Trap

Monster Type: —

Attribute:
Trap

Level: —

ATK: —

DEF: —

Rarity: Super Rare

Negates the activation of a Spell Card that designates 1 Monster as a target and destroys the Spell Card.

LON-082 Skull Lair

Card Type:
Trap

Monster Type: —

Attribute:
Trap

Level: —

ATK: —

DEF: —

Rarity: Common

Remove any number of cards in your Graveyard from play. Destroy 1 face-up Monster on the Field whose Level Stars are equal to the number of the cards you removed from play.

LON-083 Graverobber's Retribution

Card Type:
Trap

Monster Type: —

Attribute:
Trap

Level: —

ATK: —

DEF: —

Rarity: Common

During each of your Standby Phases, inflict 100 points of Direct Damage to your opponent's Life Points for each of your opponent's Monster Cards that have been removed from play.

LON-084 Deal of Phantom

Card Type:
Trap

Monster Type: —

Attribute:
Trap

Level: —

ATK: —

DEF: —

Rarity: Common

Select 1 Monster face-up on the Field. Increase the selected Monster's ATK by 100 points for each Monster in your Graveyard during the turn this card is activated. The number of Monster is applied when this card is activated.

LON-085 Destruction Punch

Card Type:
Trap

Monster Type: —

Attribute:
Trap

Level: —

ATK: —

DEF: —

Rarity:
Rare

When the ATK of an attacking Monster on your opponent's side of the Field is lower than the DEF of the attacked Defense Position Monster on your side of the Field, destroy the attacking Monster. Damage calculation is applied normally.

LON-086 Blind Destruction

Card Type:
Trap

Monster Type: —

Attribute:
Trap

Level: —

ATK: —

DEF: —

Rarity: Common

During your Standby Phase, roll 1 six-sided die once. Destroy any Monsters whose Level Stars are equal to the number rolled. If the number is "6", destroy all face-up Level 6 or higher Monsters on the Field.

LON-087 The Emperor's Holiday

Card Type:
Trap

Monster Type: —

Attribute:
Trap

Level: —

ATK: —

DEF: —

Rarity: Common

Negate the effects of all Equip Spell Cards.

LON-088 Destiny Board

Card Type:
Trap

Monster Type: —

Attribute:
Trap

Level: —

ATK: —

DEF: —

Rarity: Ultra Rare

At the end of each of your opponent's turns, place 1 "Spirit Message" card from your hand or your Deck face-up to the Field. If it is from your Deck, then shuffle your Deck. If "Spirit Message" cards "I", "N", "A" and "L" are all on the Field in their proper order, you are declared the winner. If any of the cards are destroyed or removed from the Field while constructing the message, they are all sent to your Graveyard immediately.

Card Catalog

LON-089 Spirit Message "I"

Card Type: **Spell**
Monster Type: —
Attribute: **Spell**
Level: —
ATK: —
DEF: —
Rarity: **Rare**

This card can only be placed on the Field when "Destiny Board" is active.

LON-090 Spirit Message "N"

Card Type: **Spell**
Monster Type: —
Attribute: **Spell**
Level: —
ATK: —
DEF: —
Rarity: **Rare**

This card can only be placed on the Field when "Destiny Board" is active.

LON-091 Spirit Message "A"

Card Type: **Spell**
Monster Type: —
Attribute: **Spell**
Level: —
ATK: —
DEF: —
Rarity: **Rare**

This card can only be placed on the Field when "Destiny Board" is active.

LON-092 Spirit Message "L"

Card Type: **Spell**
Monster Type: —
Attribute: **Spell**
Level: —
ATK: —
DEF: —
Rarity: **Rare**

This card can only be placed on the Field when "Destiny Board" is active.

LON-093 The Dark Door

Card Type: **Spell**
Monster Type: —
Attribute: **Spell**
Level: —
ATK: —
DEF: —
Rarity: **Common**

Both players can only attack with 1 Monster during their respective Battle Phases.

LON-094 Spiritualism

Card Type: **Spell**
Monster Type: —
Attribute: **Spell**
Level: —
ATK: —
DEF: —
Rarity: **Rare**

Return 1 Spell or Trap Card on your opponent's side of the Field to his/her hand. This card's activation and effect cannot be negated by any other card.

LON-095 Cyclon Laser

Card Type: **Equip Spell Card**
Monster Type: —
Attribute: **Spell**
Level: —
ATK: —
DEF: —
Rarity: **Common**

This card can only be used to equip "Gradius." Increases the ATK of "Gradius" by 300 points. When "Gradius" attacks with an ATK that is higher than the DEF of your opponent's Defense Position Monster, inflict the difference as Battle Damage to your opponent's Life Points.

LON-096 Bait Doll

Card Type: **Spell**
Monster Type: —
Attribute: **Spell**
Level: —
ATK: —
DEF: —
Rarity: **Common**

Force the activation of 1 face-down Trap Card. If the timing of the activation of the Trap Card is incorrect, negate the effect and destroy it. If it is not a Trap Card, it is returned to its original position. After this card is activated, it is placed into the Deck (not the Graveyard). The Deck is then shuffled.

81

LON-097 De-Fusion

Card Type: **Spell**

Monster Type: —

Attribute: **Spell**

Level: —

ATK: —

DEF: —

Rarity: **Super Rare**

Return 1 Fusion Monster Card on the Field to the Fusion Deck. In addition, if all the Fusion-Material Monsters for the returned Fusion Monster Card are in your Graveyard, you can Special Summon them all to the Field in face-up Attack or Defense Position.

LON-098 Fusion Gate

Card Type: **Spell**

Monster Type: —

Attribute: **Spell**

Level: —

ATK: —

DEF: —

Rarity: **Common**

As long as this card remains face-up on the Field, a Fusion Monster can be Special Summoned without using "Polymerization." The Fusion-Material Monsters used in the Fusion are not sent to the Graveyard, but are removed from play.

LON-099 Ekibyo Drakmord

Card Type: **Equip Spell Card**

Monster Type: —

Attribute: **Spell**

Level: —

ATK: —

DEF: —

Rarity: **Common**

A Monster equipped with this card cannot attack. Destroys the equipped Monster at the end of the 2nd turn of the player controlling the Monster. At that time, this card is returned to the owner's hand.

LON-100 Miracle Dig

Card Type: **Spell**

Monster Type: —

Attribute: **Spell**

Level: —

ATK: —

DEF: —

Rarity: **Common**

If there are 5 or more of your Monsters that have been removed from play in the current Duel, return 3 of them to the Graveyard.

LON-101 Dragonic Attack

Card Type: **Spell**

Monster Type: —

Attribute: **Spell**

Level: —

ATK: —

DEF: —

Rarity: **Common**

This card can only be used to equip Warrior-Type Monsters. The equipped Monster is treated as Dragon-Type and increases the ATK and DEF of the equipped Monster by 500 points.

LON-102 Spirit Elimination

Card Type: **Spell**

Monster Type: —

Attribute: **Spell**

Level: —

ATK: —

DEF: —

Rarity: **Common**

When Monsters in the Graveyard are removed from play, remove Monsters on your side of the Field from play as substitutes. This card remains active until the end of the turn that it is activated. The substitutes remain removed from play.

LON-103 Vengeful Bog Spirit

Card Type: **Spell**

Monster Type: —

Attribute: **Spell**

Level: —

ATK: —

DEF: —

Rarity: **Common**

All Monsters on the Field cannot attack in the same turn that they are Summoned (includes Flip Summon and Special Summon).

LON-104 Magic Cylinder

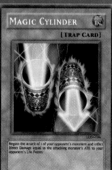

Card Type: **Trap**

Monster Type: —

Attribute: **Trap**

Level: —

ATK: —

DEF: —

Rarity: **Secret Rare**

Negate the attack of 1 of your opponent's Monsters and inflict Direct Damage equal to the attacking Monster's ATK to your opponent's Life Points.

LON-000 Gemini Elf

Card Type: **Normal Monster**

Monster Type: **Spellcaster**

Attribute: **Earth**

Level: 4

ATK: 1900

DEF: 900

Rarity: **Secret Rare**

Elf twins that alternate their attacks.

Dark Duel Stories

DDS-001 Blue-Eyes White Dragon

Card Type: Normal Monster
Monster Type: Dragon
Attribute: Light
Level: 8
ATK: 3000
DEF: 2500
Rarity: Common

Kaiba's favorite Monster is the most powerful Normal Monster Card. Destroying "Blue-Eyes" without a Spell Card will be difficult!

DDS-002 Dark Magician

Card Type: Normal Monster
Monster Type: Spellcaster
Attribute: Dark
Level: 7
ATK: 2500
DEF: 2100
Rarity: Common

A high-ranking magician of the Spellcaster-Type, the "Dark Magician" is very dangerous unless you destroy him as soon as your opponent places him on the Field.

DDS-003 Exodia the Forbidden One

Card Type: Effect Monster
Monster Type: Spellcaster
Attribute: Dark
Level: 3
ATK: 1000
DEF: 1000
Rarity: Common

This is one of the five parts necessary to resurrect "Exodia the Forbidden One."

DDS-004 Seiyaryu

Card Type: Normal Monster
Monster Type: Dragon
Attribute: Light
Level: 7
ATK: 2500
DEF: 2300
Rarity: Common

"Seiyaryu" has the same ATK as "Dark Magician." Use this Monster when the situation requires!

DDS-005 Acid Trap Hole

Card Type: Trap
Monster Type: —
Attribute: Trap
Level: —
ATK: —
DEF: —
Rarity: Common

You can use this Trap Card on face-down Monsters. Most Monsters have low DEF, so this card is very useful!

DDS-006 Salamandra

Card Type: Spell
Monster Type: —
Attribute: Spell
Level: —
ATK: —
DEF: —
Rarity: Common

Power up your FIRE Monsters with "Salamandra!"

The Eternal Duelist Soul

EDS-001 Exchange

Card Type: Spell
Monster Type: —
Attribute: Spell
Level: —
ATK: —
DEF: —
Rarity: Common

Take your opponent's powerful Spell Card, such as "Raigeki." Use this card when you have nothing useful in your hand.

EDS-002 Graceful Dice

Card Type: Spell
Monster Type: —
Attribute: Spell
Level: —
ATK: —
DEF: —
Rarity: Common

The ATK and DEF of all your Monsters will increase depending on what you roll.

EDS-003 Skull Dice

Card Type: Trap
Monster Type: —
Attribute: Trap
Level: —
ATK: —
DEF: —
Rarity: Common

The ATK and DEF of all your opponent's Monsters will decrease depending on what you roll.

Collector Tins

BPT-001 Dark Magician

Card Type: Normal Monster
Monster Type: Spellcaster
Attribute: Dark
Level: 7
ATK: 2500
DEF: 2100
Rarity: Common

A high-ranking magician of the Spellcaster-Type, the "Dark Magician" is very dangerous unless you destroy him as soon as your opponent places him on the Field.

BPT-002 Summoned Skull

Card Type: Normal Monster
Monster Type: Fiend
Attribute: Dark
Level: 6
ATK: 2500
DEF: 1200
Rarity: Common

Though "Summoned Skull" is a high-level Fiend, it's easy to Summon and extremely useful.

BPT-003 Blue-Eyes White Dragon

Card Type: Normal Monster
Monster Type: Dragon
Attribute: Light
Level: 8
ATK: 3000
DEF: 2500
Rarity: Common

Kaiba's favorite Monster is the most powerful Normal Monster Card. Destroying "Blue-Eyes" without a Spell Card will be difficult!

BPT-004 Lord of D.

Card Type: Effect Monster
Monster Type: Spellcaster
Attribute: Dark
Level: 4
ATK: 1200
DEF: 1100
Rarity: Common

"Lord of D." can protect all Dragons, but that's not all! Using "Lord of D." with "The Flute of Summoning Dragon" forms a devastating combo!

BPT-005 Red-Eyes B. Dragon

Card Type: Normal Monster
Monster Type: Dragon
Attribute: Dark
Level: 7
ATK: 2400
DEF: 2000
Rarity: Common

Joey received this rare card by defeating "Rex Raptor." This Monster can become even stronger if it fused with another Monster by "Polymerization!"

BPT-006 B. Skull Dragon

Card Type: Fusion Monster
Monster Type: Dragon
Attribute: Dark
Level: 9
ATK: 3200
DEF: 2500
Rarity: Common

Create one of the fiercest Monsters in action by fusing "Summoned Skull" and "Red-Eyes B. Dragon" with "Polymerization." This must-have card has capabilities for powerful combos.

Tournament Pack #1

TP1-001 Mechanicalchaser

Card Type: Normal Monster
Monster Type: Machine
Attribute: Dark
Level: 4
ATK: 1850
DEF: 800
Rarity: Ultra Rare

This Machine was created with only offense in mind. Don't think about defending; just attack!

TP1-002 Axe Raider

Card Type: Normal Monster
Monster Type: Warrior
Attribute: Earth
Level: 4
ATK: 1700
DEF: 1150
Rarity: Super Rare

With greater ATK than "Beautiful Headhuntress," this Warrior can change the course of battle.

TP1-003 Kwagar Hercules

Card Type: Fusion Monster
Monster Type: Insect
Attribute: Earth
Level: 6
ATK: 1900
DEF: 1700
Rarity: Super Rare

It has lower DEF than "Hercules Beetle," but it has higher ATK.

TP1-004 Patrol Robo

Card Type: Effect Monster
Monster Type: Machine
Attribute: Earth
Level: 3
ATK: 1100
DEF: 900
Rarity: Super Rare

Even if the face-down card is an Effect Monster, since you are only looking at it, the effect doesn't activate.

TP1-005 White Hole

Card Type: Trap
Monster Type: —
Attribute: Trap
Level: —
ATK: —
DEF: —
Rarity: Super Rare

If you have this Trap Card, you don't have to be afraid of "Dark Hole!"

TP1-006 Elf's Light

Card Type: Spell
Monster Type: —
Attribute: Spell
Level: —
ATK: —
DEF: —
Rarity: Rare

If you use this card with "Rogue Doll," its low DEF will become even lower. Use this card wisely.

TP1-007 Steel Shell

Card Type: Spell
Monster Type: —
Attribute: Spell
Level: —
ATK: —
DEF: —
Rarity: Rare

WATER Monsters generally have high DEF, so you can use this card without worry.

TP1-008 Blue Medicine

Card Type: Spell
Monster Type: —
Attribute: Spell
Level: —
ATK: —
DEF: —
Rarity: Rare

After drinking this blue liquid, you can taste its power in your mouth, and you gain 400 Life Points.

TP1-009 Raimei

Card Type: Spell
Monster Type: —
Attribute: Spell
Level: —
ATK: —
DEF: —
Rarity: Rare

Lightning falls from the sky and strikes your opponent for 300 Life Points of damage.

TP1-010 Burning Spear

Card Type: Spell
Monster Type: —
Attribute: Spell
Level: —
ATK: —
DEF: —
Rarity: Rare

This Spell Card is important for FIRE Monsters.

TP1-011 Gust Fan

Card Type: Spell
Monster Type: —
Attribute: Spell
Level: —
ATK: —
DEF: —
Rarity: Rare

This mysterious fan strengthens WIND Monsters, which is useful because there are many Monsters that counteract Winged Beasts.

TP1-012 Tiger Axe

Card Type: Normal Monster
Monster Type: Beast-Warrior
Attribute: Earth
Level: 4
ATK: 1300
DEF: 1100
Rarity: Rare

This strong Beast-Warrior's trademark is its huge axe in its hand.

TP1-013 Goddess with the Third Eye

Card Type: Effect Monster
Monster Type: Fairy
Attribute: Light
Level: 4
ATK: 1200
DEF: 1000
Rarity: Rare

They say her third eye can see the truth. Out of Monsters that can substitute as a Fusion-Material Monster, this card has very high ATK. When the Fusion-Material Monsters you need have low Attack and DEF, use this card instead. "Goddess with the Third Eye" is also decent in battle.

TP1-014 Beastking of the Swamps

Card Type: Effect Monster
Monster Type: Aqua
Attribute: Water
Level: 4
ATK: 1000
DEF: 1100
Rarity: Rare

This Monster lives in bottomless swamps. Out of Monsters that can substitute as a Fusion-Material Monster, this card has very high DEF. However, 1100 DEF is still low, so you'll need other cards to power it up or use "Umi" Field Spell Card.

TP1-015 Versago the Destroyer

Card Type: Effect Monster
Monster Type: Fiend
Attribute: Dark
Level: 3
ATK: 1100
DEF: 900
Rarity: Rare

"Versago the Destroyer" materializes in a spooky light and destroys everything around it. Fiend-Type or DARK Monsters are very useful. It's easy to create a Deck that is full of DARK Monsters, so include this card as a Fusion-Material Monster.

TP1-016 Oscillo Hero #2

Card Type: Normal Monster
Monster Type: Thunder
Attribute: Light
Level: 3
ATK: 1000
DEF: 500
Rarity: Common

This strange electric child does a weird dance to shoot out lightning bolts.

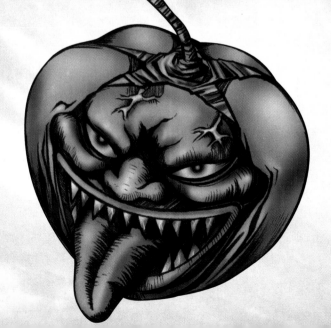

TP1-017 Giant Flea

Card Type: Normal Monster
Monster Type: Insect
Attribute: Earth
Level: 4
ATK: 1500
DEF: 1200
Rarity: Common

"Giant Flea" has high Attack Power, but sometimes, it jumps too high and hits its head.

TP1-018 Bean Soldier

Card Type: Normal Monster
Monster Type: Plant
Attribute: Earth
Level: 4
ATK: 1400
DEF: 1300
Rarity: Common

This useful Plant becomes very flavorful when it takes a shower.

TP1-019 The Statue of Easter Island

Card Type: Normal Monster
Monster Type: Rock
Attribute: Earth
Level: 4
ATK: 1100
DEF: 1400
Rarity: Common

When these statues were created is a source of great discussion. Its thin eyes glow blue-white.

TP1-020 Corroding Shark

Card Type: Normal Monster
Monster Type: Zombie
Attribute: Dark
Level: 3
ATK: 1100
DEF: 700
Rarity: Common

This Monster doesn't realize that it has passed away. Many different animals live inside its stomach.

TP1-021 Wow Warrior

Card Type: Normal Monster
Monster Type: Fish
Attribute: Water
Level: 4
ATK: 1250
DEF: 900
Rarity: Common

This Warrior can also fight on land, though its scales aren't very protective.

TP1-022 Winged Dragon, Guardian of the Fortress #2

Card Type: Normal Monster
Monster Type: Winged Beast
Attribute: Wind
Level: 4
ATK: 1200
DEF: 1000
Rarity: Common

This secondary Winged-Beast becomes more useful when combined with "Mountain."

TP1-023 Oscillo Hero

Card Type: Normal Monster
Monster Type: Warrior
Attribute: Earth
Level: 3
ATK: 1250
DEF: 700
Rarity: Common

When it meets a lady, for some reason, it shows off its cape.

TP1-024 Shining Friendship

Card Type: Normal Monster
Monster Type: Fairy
Attribute: Light
Level: 4
ATK: 1300
DEF: 1100
Rarity: Common

When it sees anything big and round, "Shining Friendship" approaches it, thinking that it's a friend. When it realizes its mistake, it flees.

TP1-025 Hercules Beetle

Card Type: Normal Monster
Monster Type: Insect
Attribute: Earth
Level: 5
ATK: 1500
DEF: 2000
Rarity: Common

This beetle has high ATK and DEF. Decide whether to Tribute Summon this Monster or use it for Fusion.

TP1-026 The Judgment Hand

Card Type:
Normal Monster

Monster Type:
Warrior

Attribute:
Earth

Level: 3

ATK: 1400

DEF: 700

Rarity: Common

With its powerful fist, it can knock out a weakling in a single blow! However, it's weak at defense.

TP1-027 Wodan the Resident of the Forest

Card Type:
Effect Monster

Monster Type:
Warrior

Attribute:
Earth

Level: 3

ATK: 900

DEF: 1200

Rarity: Common

This card is effective in a Plant-Type Deck, but its basic ATK and DEF are low, so it is not very useful.

TP1-028 Cyber Soldier of Darkworld

Card Type:
Normal Monster

Monster Type:
Machine

Attribute:
Dark

Level: 4

ATK: 1400

DEF: 1200

Rarity: Common

Though this Machine moves using shadow energy, it's not as strong as Fiends and Spellcasters who can truly harness the power of the shadows.

TP1-029 Cockroach Knight

Card Type:
Effect Monster

Monster Type:
Insect

Attribute:
Earth

Level: 3

ATK: 800

DEF: 900

Rarity: Common

This card will always be in your Deck or hand.

TP1-030 Kuwagata α

Card Type:
Normal Monster

Monster Type:
Insect

Attribute:
Earth

Level: 4

ATK: 1250

DEF: 1000

Rarity: Common

This powerful Insect is Fusion-Material for Summoning "Kwagar Hercules."

Tournament Pack #2

TP2-001 Morphing Jar

Card Type: Effect Monster
Monster Type: Rock
Attribute: Earth
Level: 2
ATK: 700
DEF: 600
Rarity: Ultra Rare

You can create Decks that focus on this card as its centerpiece. This card is very useful when you have no useful cards in your hand while your opponent has powerful cards in hand.

TP2-002 Dragon Seeker

Card Type: Effect Monster
Monster Type: Fiend
Attribute: Dark
Level: 6
ATK: 2000
DEF: 2100
Rarity: Super Rare

Not only is "Dragon Seeker's" effect somewhat useful, but its ATK and DEF are high. If everything goes according to plan, you can use its effect to destroy a powerful Dragon, then you can attack your opponent.

TP2-003 Giant Red Seasnake

Card Type: Normal Monster
Monster Type: Aqua
Attribute: Water
Level: 4
ATK: 1800
DEF: 800
Rarity: Super Rare

This sea snake is one of the most powerful Aqua-Type Monsters. If you power this card up with Spell Cards, then it will be unstoppable!

TP2-004 Exile of the Wicked

Card Type: Spell
Monster Type: —
Attribute: Spell
Level: —
ATK: —
DEF: —
Rarity: Super Rare

Having lost his wife and children to Fiends, he discovered a Spell to counteract Fiends. This eerie Spell scares everyone. Fiend-Type Monsters are generally very powerful, especially "Summoned Skull." However, if your opponent does not play Fiend Monsters, then this card is useless.

TP2-005 Call of the Grave

Card Type: Trap
Monster Type: —
Attribute: Trap
Level: —
ATK: —
DEF: —
Rarity: Super Rare

Use this card when your opponent is about to revive a powerful Monster. Timing is essential.

TP2-006 Mikazukinoyaiba

Card Type: Normal Monster
Monster Type: Dragon
Attribute: Dark
Level: 7
ATK: 2200
DEF: 2350
Rarity: Rare

This high-level Monster has high defense points. It is a DARK Monster, just like "Red-Eyes B. Dragon."

TP2-007 Skull Guardian

Card Type: Ritual Monster
Monster Type: Warrior
Attribute: Light
Level: 7
ATK: 2050
DEF: 2500
Rarity: Rare

"Skull Guardian" can be counted on to protect the king. With 2500 DEF, ordinary attacks won't hurt it!

TP2-008 Novox's Prayer

Card Type: Spell
Monster Type: —
Attribute: Spell
Level: —
ATK: —
DEF: —
Rarity: Rare

You need this card to Summon the Ritual Monster "Skull Guardian." This card is useless by itself, so make sure to get both cards!

TRADING CARD GAME

TP2-009 Dokurorider

Card Type:
Ritual Monster

Monster Type:
Zombie

Attribute:
Dark

Level: 6

ATK: 1900

DEF: 1850

Rarity: Rare

This legendary Monster is a Special Summon, so it cannot be destroyed by "Trap Hole." Also, you can Normal Summon another Monster on the same turn "Dokurorider" is Summoned, increasing the Monsters on your Field.

TP2-010 Revival of Dokurorider

Card Type:
Spell

Monster Type: —

Attribute:
Spell

Level: —

ATK: —

DEF: —

Rarity: Rare

You need this card to Summon the Ritual Monster "Dokurorider." This card is useless by itself, so make sure to get both cards!

TP2-011 Beautiful Headhuntress

Card Type:
Normal Monster

Monster Type:
Warrior

Attribute:
Earth

Level: 4

ATK: 1600

DEF: 800

Rarity: Rare

This beautiful woman sharpens her blade everyday. However, she is weak at defending.

TP2-012 Sonic Maid

Card Type:
Normal Monster

Monster Type:
Warrior

Attribute:
Earth

Level: 3

ATK: 1200

DEF: 900

Rarity: Rare

"Sonic Maid" isn't very strong on her own, but when fused, she becomes "Warrior of Tradition!"

TP2-013 Mystical Sheep #1

Card Type:
Effect Monster

Monster Type:
Beast

Attribute:
Earth

Level: 3

ATK: 1150

DEF: 900

Rarity: Rare

The coin on the tip of its tail puts its enemies to sleep. This card is more useful as a Fusion-Material Monster if it is protected by using "Sogen" to power it up.

TP2-014 Warrior of Tradition

Card Type:
Fusion Monster

Monster Type:
Warrior

Attribute:
Earth

Level: 6

ATK: 1900

DEF: 1700

Rarity: Rare

Though this kimono beauty can be rough, her ATK are high to be useful in battle.

TP2-015 Soul of the Pure

Card Type:
Spell

Monster Type: —

Attribute:
Spell

Level: —

ATK: —

DEF: —

Rarity: Common

A fairy uses her own life essence to heal people.

TP2-016 Dancing Elf

Card Type:
Normal Monster

Monster Type:
Fairy

Attribute:
Wind

Level: 1

ATK: 300

DEF: 200

Rarity: Common

Though this elf is beautiful, she has low ATK and DEF, so she may be only useful in Fairy-Type Decks.

Card Catalog

TP2-017 Turu-Purun

Card Type: Normal Monster
Monster Type: Aqua
Attribute: Water
Level: 2
ATK: 450
DEF: 500
Rarity: Common

"Turu-Purun's" large stomach is cool to the touch, so if you rest your face against it, it feels refreshing!

TP2-018 Dharma Cannon

Card Type: Normal Monster
Monster Type: Machine
Attribute: Dark
Level: 2
ATK: 900
DEF: 500
Rarity: Common

"Dharma Cannon" has various weapons all over its body, but it still has low ATK....

TP2-019 Stuffed Animal

Card Type: Normal Monster
Monster Type: Warrior
Attribute: Earth
Level: 3
ATK: 1200
DEF: 900
Rarity: Common

This Monster never attacks people who really love stuffed animals.

TP2-020 Spirit of the Books

Card Type: Normal Monster
Monster Type: Winged Beast
Attribute: Wind
Level: 4
ATK: 1400
DEF: 1200
Rarity: Common

"Spirit of the Books" has no strengths of weaknesses. It attacks using different battle strategies, but its lack of firsthand knowledge is its downfall.

TP2-021 Faith Bird

Card Type: Normal Monster
Monster Type: Winged Beast
Attribute: Wind
Level: 4
ATK: 1500
DEF: 1100
Rarity: Common

If you're lost in the mountains at night, "Faith Bird" comes to your rescue as long as you're human.

TP2-022 Takuhee

Card Type: Normal Monster
Monster Type: Winged Beast
Attribute: Wind
Level: 4
ATK: 1450
DEF: 1000
Rarity: Common

This bird can be useful in various situations due to its decent ATK.

TP2-023 Maiden of the Moonlight

Card Type: Normal Monster
Monster Type: Spellcaster
Attribute: Light
Level: 4
ATK: 1500
DEF: 1300
Rarity: Common

If you take a moonlight swim in the forest, you have a chance to meet this maiden. If you whistle, she will smile.

TP2-024 Queen of Autumn Leaves

Card Type: Normal Monster
Monster Type: Plant
Attribute: Earth
Level: 5
ATK: 1800
DEF: 1500
Rarity: Common

In the calm late afternoon, she relaxes by drinking tea with her husband "Green Phantom King."

TP2-025 Two-Headed King Rex

Card Type: Normal Monster
Monster Type: Dinosaur
Attribute: Earth
Level: 4
ATK: 1600
DEF: 1200
Rarity: Common

This Dinosaur attacks with its two heads simultaneously.

TP2-026 Garoozis

Card Type:
Normal Monster

Monster Type:
Beast-Warrior

Attribute:
Fire

Level: 5

ATK: 1800

DEF: 1500

Rarity: Common

"Garoozis" has the head of a dragon and swings an axe with tremendous strength. However, he cannot defend as well.

TP2-027 Crawling Dragon #2

Card Type:
Normal Monster

Monster Type:
Dinosaur

Attribute:
Earth

Level: 4

ATK: 1600

DEF: 1200

Rarity: Common

Its jaws are so powerful that there's nothing in existence that cannot be torn to shreds by its fangs.

TP2-028 Parrot Dragon

Card Type:
Normal Monster

Monster Type:
Dragon

Attribute:
Wind

Level: 5

ATK: 2000

DEF: 1300

Rarity: Common

This cute and comical Dragon actually thirsts for the taste of destruction.

TP2-029 Sky Dragon

Card Type:
Normal Monster

Monster Type:
Dragon

Attribute:
Wind

Level: 6

ATK: 1900

DEF: 1800

Rarity: Common

With four wings, this Dragon looks more like a bird. Its sharp wings can even cut through diamonds!

TP2-030 Water Magician

Card Type:
Normal Monster

Monster Type:
Aqua

Attribute:
Water

Level: 4

ATK: 1400

DEF: 1000

Rarity: Common

"Water Magician" can control water and drown her enemies.

McDonald Promotion

MP1-001 Millennium Shield

Card Type: Normal Monster
Monster Type: Warrior
Attribute: Earth
Level: 5
ATK: 0
DEF: 3000
Rarity: Ultra Rare

Even "Blue-Eyes White Dragon" cannot destroy "Millennium Shield" in Defense Position. Use this card to buy yourself some time.

MP1-002 Cosmo Queen

Card Type: Normal Monster
Monster Type: Spellcaster
Attribute: Dark
Level: 8
ATK: 2900
DEF: 2450
Rarity: Ultra Rare

This Spellcaster has higher ATK than "Dark Magician!"

MP1-003 Goddess of Whim

Card Type: Effect Monster
Monster Type: Fairy
Attribute: Light
Level: 3
ATK: 950
DEF: 700
Rarity: Super Rare

Not many Effect Monster cards utilize a coin flip. If you're successful, "Goddess of Whim" has 1900 ATK!

MP1-004 Frog the Jam

Card Type: Normal Monster
Monster Type: Aqua
Attribute: Water
Level: 2
ATK: 700
DEF: 500
Rarity: Common

Though it has low ATK and DEF, it's useful for offering as a Tribute.

MP1-005 Yaranzo

Card Type: Normal Monster
Monster Type: Zombie
Attribute: Dark
Level: 4
ATK: 1300
DEF: 1500
Rarity: Common

"Yaranzo" usually hides inside a treasure chest and waits for its next victim.

MP1-006 Takriminos

Card Type: Normal Monster
Monster Type: Sea Serpent
Attribute: Water
Level: 4
ATK: 1500
DEF: 1200
Rarity: Super Rare

It has high ATK and DEF for a Monster that is very easy to Summon.

MP1-007 Stuffed Animal

Card Type: Normal Monster
Monster Type: Warrior
Attribute: Earth
Level: 3
ATK: 1200
DEF: 900
Rarity: Common

This Monster never attacks people who really love stuffed animals.

MP1-008 Megasonic Eye

Card Type: Normal Monster
Monster Type: Machine
Attribute: Dark
Level: 5
ATK: 1500
DEF: 1800
Rarity: Common

A strange Machine with high DEF, this card is hard to use because you need to offer another Monster as a Tribute to Summon "Megasonic Eye."

MP1-009 Yamadron

Card Type: Normal Monster
Monster Type: Dragon
Attribute: Fire
Level: 5
ATK: 1600
DEF: 1800
Rarity: Common

"Yamadron" is a FIRE Dragon that has higher ATK than "Megasonic Eye." Its three heads get along great.

MP1-010 Three-Legged Zombies

Card Type: Normal Monster
Monster Type: Zombie
Attribute: Dark
Level: 3
ATK: 1100
DEF: 800
Rarity: Common

Two strange Zombies only have the strength of one. Since it can't move around easily, it has low DEF....

MP1-011 Flying Penguin

Card Type: Normal Monster
Monster Type: Aqua
Attribute: Water
Level: 4
ATK: 1200
DEF: 1000
Rarity: Common

Not many have ever seen "Flying Penguin." It is usually calm, but when angered, watch out!

MP1-012 Fairy's Gift

Card Type: Normal Monster
Monster Type: Spellcaster
Attribute: Light
Level: 4
ATK: 1400
DEF: 1000
Rarity: Common

If you power up "Fairy's Gift" with Spell Cards, then it can be very useful.

MP1-013 Ushi Oni

Card Type: Normal Monster
Monster Type: Fiend
Attribute: Dark
Level: 6
ATK: 2150
DEF: 1950
Rarity: Common

Dark magic resurrected this cow Fiend, but for some reason, it comes out of a pot. "Ushi Oni" is quite useful for a Monster that needs only one Monster as a Tribute.

MP1-014 Turtle Bird

Card Type: Normal Monster
Monster Type: Aqua
Attribute: Water
Level: 6
ATK: 1900
DEF: 1700
Rarity: Common

In the air, hunters aim for "Turtle Bird." In the sea, fisherman hunt "Turtle Bird." Isn't there a place in the world safe for this creature?

MP1-015 Dark-Piercing Light

Card Type: Spell
Monster Type: —
Attribute: Spell
Level: —
ATK: —
DEF: —
Rarity: Super Rare

Use this card when you think your opponent is Setting Flip Effect Monsters to force them to activate before you Summon a Key Monster.

Shonen Jump

JMP-001 Blue-Eyes White Dragon

Card Type: Normal Monster
Monster Type: Dragon
Attribute: Light
Level: 8
Attack Points: 3000
Defense Points: 2500
Rarity: Common

Kaiba's favorite Monster is the most powerful Normal Monster Card. Destroying "Blue-Eyes" without a Spell Card will be difficult!